The Masterworks of Literature Series

SYLVIA E. BOWMAN, *Editor*
Indiana University

Mark Twain's Quarrel with Heaven

Mark Twain's Quarrel with Heaven

"Captain Stormfield's Visit to Heaven"
And Other Sketches

by MARK TWAIN

Edited for the Modern Reader by
Ray B. Browne
BOWLING GREEN UNIVERSITY

COLLEGE & UNIVERSITY PRESS · *Publishers*
NEW HAVEN, CONN.

Copyright © 1970 by
College and University Press Services, Inc.
All Rights Reserved

Library of Congress Catalog Card Number: 75-106984

New Material, Introduction and Notes
by RAY B. BROWNE

MANUFACTURED IN THE UNITED STATES OF AMERICA BY
UNITED PRINTING SERVICES, INC.
NEW HAVEN, CONN.

TO LEON HOWARD
FRIEND

Acknowledgments

The research for this volume was made possible by a grant from the American Philosophical Society, and the work completed during a lull in teaching made possible by the generosity of the Purdue Research Foundation. I would like to express the appreciation of all Twain researchers who have worked with Professor Henry Nash Smith and Mr. Frederick Anderson, Literary Executor of the Mark Twain Papers, for their helpful suggestions and unstinting services. I should like also to express my appreciation to Mrs. Matthew Josephson, Librarian of the American Academy of Arts and Letters, for invaluable assistance; and to my colleagues Professor Martin Light and John S. Tuckey for assistance with the manuscript. Lastly but most importantly I should like to express in public the appreciation I have so often stated in private to my wife, Pat, and my little Huck Finns, Glenn, Kevin, and Alicia: no one knows better than she and they the price of scholarship.

Note: All material in this volume written by Mark Twain, not hitherto published, is copyrighted by The Mark Twain Company 1970.

Contents

Introduction	11
References to Introduction	32

Part I
Captain Stormfield's Visit to Heaven	39

Part II
"The Late Reverend Sam Jones's Reception in Heaven"	111

Part III
"Mental Telegraphy?"	117
Appendix A: Old Abe's "Slap" at Chicago	121
Appendix B: Alternate Passage	123

Introduction

THE QUESTION of the hereafter worried Mark Twain throughout life. Son of a tender-hearted Presbyterian mother, he was reared in the shadow of the Old Ship of Zion Sunday School in his hometown of Hannibal, Missouri. But he inherited his agnostic father's independence of mind and his recalcitrance at being a follower in anything—especially in his family's "pious joys." Because of the resulting tug-of-war between heart and head, Twain never felt secure or comfortable.

His feelings about supernatural powers were ambivalent. "Neither Howells nor I believe in hell or the divinity of the Saviour—but no matter, the Saviour is none the less a sacred Personage," he wrote his brother Orion on March 23, 1878. Twenty years later, in a passage in his Notebooks hitherto unpublished, Twain belittled Christ's sacrifice in dying on the Cross. It was nothing for Him to suffer a few hours, less than a woman undergoes in childbirth, when He knew that He would subsequently go to heaven. Christ may have brought eternal life into the world, but He also brought eternal misery. Christ was despicable in always seeking praise for His deeds, "fishing for compliments," as Twain called it.[1] In his last days Twain thought the whole idea of Christ a "myth": "There have been Saviours in every age of the world. It is all just a fairy tale, like the idea of Santa Claus."[2] Nevertheless, Jesus was superior to His earthly followers, Twain wrote in his Notebooks: "As concerns Christ there are some uncertainties but for our solace we know one thing for sure—He was not a Christian."[3]

Twain's conclusions about Satan were even more equivocal. He once planned to write a defense of him, as the Notebooks reveal. One time Twain dreamed that he tried to sell his soul to the devil but that Satan would not buy it.

Twain explained the rejection in his Notebooks: Satan's "polite objections & evasions. Certain lines of goods he was overstocked with. Never *had* paid the prices attributed to him by lying priests."[4] In his article "Concerning the Jews," Twain wrote that, although he had no special regard for Satan, he at least had no prejudice against him and might, in fact, have leaned "a little his way on account of his not having a fair show." Twain, however, never underestimated Satan's power, as he only half humorously revealed in a Notebook entry: "Let us be grateful that Satan is not a Christian —he is plenty tough enough, just as he is."[5] The Satan whom Twain finally pictured in *The Mysterious Stranger*, his fullest statement on the subject, is by no means an object of hate.

For God—or the usual concept of Him—Twain's hatred was, however, absolute and all-pervading. Entries in his Notebooks reveal his true feelings: "God is Might. (& he is shifty, malicious & uncertain)." "I could not worship a God that made the fly." "The cowardliest thing about Bibles is that they excuse God's wickedness and condemn man's instead of being honest & turning the matter the other way around."[6]

In an extended inventory he mused once on how, given the opportunity, he would create a God who would be an improvement on the existing one:

> If I were going to construct a God (to take the place of the present one) I would furnish him with some ways & qualities & characteristics which the present One lacks.
> He would not stoop to *ask* for any man's compliments, praises, flatteries; & he would be far above *exacting* them. I would have Him as self-respecting as the better sort of men in these regards.
> He would not be a merchant, a trader. He would not buy these things.
> He would not sell, or offer to sell, temporary benefits or the joys of eternity for the product called worship. I would

have Him as dignified as the better sort of men in this regard.
He would value no love but the love born of kindnesses conferred; not that born of benevolence contracted for.
Repentance in a man's heart for a wrong done would cancel & annul that sin, & no verbal prayers for forgiveness be required or desired or expected of that man.
In His Bible there would be no Unforgivable Sin. He would recognize in Himself the Author & Inventor of Sin, & Author & Inventor of the vehicle for its commission; & would place the whole responsibility where it would of right belong: upon Himself, the only Sinner.

Still he stretched his bitter list:

> He would not be a jealous God—a trait so small that even men despise it in each other.
> He would not boast.
> He would keep private his admirations of Himself; he would regard self-praise as unbecoming the dignity of His position.
> He would not have the spirit of Vengeance in His heart; then it would not issue from His lips.
> There would not be any hell—except the one we live in from the cradle to the grave.
> There would not be any heavens—of the kind described in the world's Bibles.
> He would spend some of His eternities in trying to forgive Himself for making man unhappy when He could have made him happy with the same effort; & He would spend the rest of them in studying astronomy.[7]

Twain delighted in contemporary witticisms about hell, as the frequently repeated entries in the Notebooks reveal: "Heaven for climate, hell for society"; "The gentleman from Philadelphia said he found nothing familiar in hell but the pavement." And he positively reveled in Robert Ingersoll's tale of the Presbyterian saint who went from heaven to hell on a cheap excursion ticket and "couldn't sell his return ticket."[8] But Twain never had the comfort of his convictions: "I don't believe in hell—but I'm afraid of it," he conceded in his later years.

As to Twain's ability to write on heaven and hell, he confessed in his letter to Orion, mentioned above, that he had great difficulty thinking about hell as a subject: "I have tried, all these years, to think of some way of 'doing' hell, too—& have always had to give it up. Hell, in my book, will not occupy five pages of MS, I judge—it will be only covert hints, I suppose, & quickly dropped. I may end by not even referring to it."[9] But the idea of writing on hell continued to intrigue him. There are several projects itemized in the Notebooks, ones never developed. He probably thought about the subject in connection with *Captain Stormfield's Visit to Heaven,* for on one section of the manuscript there is the penciled notation "And Hell"; but there is no mention in the story itself other than the Captain's assurance in his own mind that he is heading for hell.

Twain's confidence in his ability to "do" heaven was, however, much stronger. He planned the project several times through the years, as undeveloped ideas in the Notebooks reveal; but in *Captain Stormfield's Visit to Heaven,* as we have it, the only reference to Christ or to God is the coy one to the head clerk at the entrance to heaven, a reference the Captain uses to help identify the Earth as "the one the Saviour saved."

I

Twain's most famous effort to "do" heaven is the remarkable *Captain Stormfield's Visit to Heaven,* that is included in this volume—a free-wheeling satire on the conventional concept of the holy destination of souls and man's behavior when he gets there.[10] This fabulous adventure of the Captain is somewhat discontinuous and repetitious because Twain worked on it for about forty years. When he died in 1910, the story was still unfinished, although the project had always lain close to his heart and intentions. As it is here printed, in the order most nearly approximating that which seems to have been the author's plans, the story begins with a brief note explaining about Stormfield. Then it moves into Chapter One, which starts with Stormfield's dying and taking flight into the next world—for hell, he assumes. On the trip out, he meets a Jew, Solomon Goldstein, against whom he is naturally prejudiced: "Christians always are, you know." But in a passage clearly reflecting Twain's sadness over the death of his favorite child, Susy, Stormfield discovers that Jews are people just like everybody else—"worse than that I cannot say of them," he observes in another instance.

In this chapter, among other adventures, Stormfield and Goldstein are joined in the flight by a Negro, Sam. About him Stormfield says: "He was a good chap, and like his race: I have seen but few niggers that hadn't their hearts in the right place." Here in plain language is Twain's attitude toward Negroes, the feeling which led him to pay the college expenses of at least one Negro because he felt it his obligation as a white man, the sympathy which drove him to create Nigger Jim in *Huckleberry Finn* (one of the great characters in literature), and the compulsion which made him so fiercely champion Negro rights that his wife, Livy, once suggested that Mark should "consider every man colored until he was proved white."

Chapter Three begins in some confusion with the introduction of a certain "Peters," who is undoubtedly an alias for Twain's close friend Reverend Joseph Twichell.[11] Stormfield begins to play around, racing comets, an activity fitting and proper; for Twain was born with the coming of Halley's Comet in 1835 and correctly forecast that he would die with its return in 1910. This section allows Twain to discuss also one of the topics which intrigued him in his later years:

[15]

the immensity of space. This chapter also includes the most artistically satisfactory part of the whole story—the scalding attack on egocentric Americans, and man in general, who feel that in the beginning God created America—and the Earth—and then rested, supremely satisfied: this country, this world and universe, have lost their importance in bigger things.

Numerous quotations from the Notebooks demonstrate the passion of Twain's feeling about nationalism: "Patriotism is being carried to insane excess. I know men who do not love God because He is a foreigner." "From man's point of view Patriotism is the noblest thing there is; from God's it is the meanest." "Mene, mene, tekel e pluribus unum—put none but Americans on guard tonight. What Tyndal said in '74 [sic]."[12] In a long, savage comment on the mutual incompatibility of patriotism and Christianity, Twain remarked:

> Patriotism is a high and holy thing. It will remain a high and holy thing, and jointly admirable and praiseworthy. Christianity will never change it. Its noble doctrine of universal brotherhood is for angels, if for anybody—it is not possible for men. Christianity cannot teach a fish to fly nor aliens to love each other. We can (all) not even imagine a *heaven* where there are no frontiers, (and) where all foreigners (are welcome, [and] are all)—including Satan's people—are brothers, and Patriotism is a vice unknown; ... By the law of his religion a Christian must labor for the breaking down of all (barriers) walls that interrupt the fusion of the race into a common brotherhood; and one of the most formidable of these is Patriotism; it marches with every frontier in the world.
> ... Not that Patriotism should cease, (but that) and not that the talk about 'universal brotherhood should cease, but that the incongruous firm be dissolved and each limb of it be required to transact business by itself for the future.[13]

INTRODUCTION

When Stormfield arrives in heaven, Twain satirizes man's imposition of his customs and mores on those of wiser beings. Man soon loses his desire for wings, halos, harps, and eternal singing. There is pain in heaven, as well as work. In short, despite its variation from expectations, Stormfield finally concludes that it is "the sensiblest heaven" it could have been.

Chapter Four begins with some repetition about the foolishness of man's trying to fly when he obviously was not built for wings. Then Stormfield moves into a section in which injustices of the Earth are corrected. A barkeeper from New York arrives expecting "all hands to turn out" to welcome him; and, since nobody in heaven is to be disappointed, all hands do come to greet him. A Tennessee tailor is treated as superior to Shakespeare and Homer, although on Earth his talent went unrecognized. A Hoboken sausage-maker, who on Earth unostentatiously gave to the poor, is knighted.

There are some "unsacrilegious things" that people expect in heaven and do not receive. For example, "a Brooklyn preacher by the name of Talmage" has been saying on Earth that the first thing he will do "when he gets to heaven, will be to fling his arms around Abraham, Isaac and Jacob, and kiss them, and weep on them." But, since millions of people on Earth have been "promising themselves the same thing" and because "as many as sixty thousand people" arrive daily, such sentimentality is clearly intolerable. This Talmage—the Reverend T. DeWitt Talmage, pastor of the Central Presbyterian Church (later Tabernacle) of Brooklyn—had been a target of Twain's barbs since 1870 when the preacher had avowed that the smell of workingmen in his congregation offended refined nostrils. Twain excoriated him in the columns of the Buffalo *Express* (1870), which he partly owned at the time, and in the monthly department he conducted for the *Galaxy* (1870). Twain's vengeance pursued Talmage even to Glory.

[17]

Chapter Five, called by Twain "Captain Stormfield Resumes" and printed here in its entirety for the first time, develops the author's near obsession with the grandness of illimitable space. After touching on such a topical subject as whether or not a dead veteran is really dead when his heirs still collect benefits from the government, Stormfield commends the Maker of heaven for having had the foresight to construct His domain large enough to accommodate the souls that will be coming for "billions and billions and billions of years" and still have ample room.

In Chapter Six, "Journey to the Asterisk," here first printed fully, Stormfield and his pal Sandy are so overwhelmed by the bigness of heaven that they can no longer abide it. Then in a Swiftean technique, Twain switches to an infinitely smaller world, an "asterisk," which is "twenty-five or thirty miles in circumference," where everything is a photographic copy of its counterpart on earth. As on earth, preachers commend their people as "the noblest work of God"; and not a single "clothes pin" has sense enough to smirk. These creatures are vitiated by the same weaknesses that enervate Earthlings, but they have one sophistication: each person can see into every other person's mind while at the same time thinking that his own is concealed from everybody else!

In Chapter Seven, "From Captain Stormfield's Reminiscences," also printed here for the first time, Twain is at his bitterest; and this section is undoubtedly a product of his last years. Stormfield's friend Sandy tells the Captain about the creation of the human being. Before this creation, there had been another race, one of immortals called in private "Holy Doughnuts" because in them good and bad qualities were evenly divided and therefore neutralized one another. But the Creators were dissatisfied with these creatures because they did not contain "*variety*." The Authorities therefore created man. But, through negligence, the moral qualities were unevenly distributed; and man was therefore "just a ragtag and bobtail Mob of nondescripts, and not worth propagating, of course."

The story as thus outlined is obviously spotty and unevenly worked out. But Twain always liked it. In 1886 he told his daughter Susy (as she recorded in her biography of him) that "the only book that he had been pertickularly anxious to write was one locked in the safe downstairs, not yet published." Twain, when reading this passage in the early 1900's, noted: "The reference here is to a MS entitled 'Captain Stormfield's Visit to Heaven.' It is still in that safe; at least it was still there ten years ago when I saw it last. . . . I have often thought of finishing it, but was probably beguiled from my half-purpose by some new and sharper interest. I am still intending to finish it, and shall probably continue in that mind indefinitely; it is one of the stabilities of my character that I am always intending to do things."[14]

On August 29, 1906, he dictated in his *Autobiography* that he was going to put the story into that work to be published in a half-century, when "I shall have been so long under the sod that I shan't care about the results." Then he added: "*Three hours later.* I have just burned the closing two-thirds of it."[15] But he, of course, had not burned any of it. The next day he continued in his *Autobiography*, with a passage never before published: "I was never willing to destroy 'Captain Stormfield's Visit to Heaven.' Now and then, in the past thirty [sic] years I have overhauled my literary stock and transferred some of it to the fire, but Stormfield's Visit always escaped. (Secretly & Privately I liked it, I couldn't help it). I am obliged to suspect that the hand of Providence was in it."[16] Although Twain ran a line through the last sentence, he probably felt that there was more truth than humor in it.

Instead of burying the story in his *Autobiography* for posterity, Twain published some two-thirds of it—the section beginning with Chapter III, "Well when I had been dead about thirty years"—as "Extracts from Captain Stormfield's Visit to Heaven" in *Harper's Magazine* for December, 1907, and January, 1908, and then as a slim book in October, 1909, only six months before his death.

II

The inception of the story was lost in the mists of Twain's memory; and, when he talked about its origin in his last years, his facts were incorrect. Twain's memory was always weak: "When I was younger I could remember anything, whether it happened or not; but I am getting old and soon I shall remember only the latter," he mused once to A. B. Paine, his friend and biographer. Twain said to him on another occasion: "It isn't so astonishing the things I can remember, as the number of things I can remember that aren't so." *Captain Stormfield* is a case in point.

In Twain's mind the story had become inseparably associated with Captain Edgar (Ned) Wakeman, the roaring, blasphemous, companionable sea captain with whom Twain had traveled from San Francisco to the Nicaraguan Isthmus in December, 1866, when he was on his way to New York, and then again from the Isthmus to San Francisco in the spring of 1868.

On the 1866 trip the ship had hardly cleared the Golden Gate when a fierce storm threatened to founder her. Many of the passengers began to pray; but one, more experienced than the others, felt consoled by Wakeman's seamanship: " 'If anybody can save her it's old Wakeman'," Twain quoted in his Notebooks. With the storm over, Twain, with his great ability to get to know people, became well acquainted with Wakeman, for whom he immediately developed great respect and fondness: "I'd rather travel with that old portly, hearty, jolly, boisterous, good-natured sailor, Capt. Ned Wakeman, than with any other man I ever came across," he wrote in his Notebooks a few days later. The Captain told Twain several stories and anecdotes that he wrote up in the next weeks and months as copy for his newsletters to the *Alta California* (1867), for which he was correspondent, and which he later used in various ways in his books: Wakeman is "Captain Waxman" in the newspaper sketches, "Captain Ned Blakely" in *Roughing It,* "Captain Hurricane Jones" in *Rambling Notes,* and "Captain Davis" in *The Great Dark.*[17]

Wakeman's influence on Twain began immediately and lasted for the remainder of Twain's life. His Notebooks, both published and unpublished, abound with references to the Captain. Generally these references are to an experience that the Captain recounted which Twain had used or planned to use. But often they are no fuller or more explicit than "Ned Wakeman," "Captain Wakeman," or "Wakeman"—not so much as though Twain were exploiting the Captain as that he was merely remembering him. Twain came to think of *Stormfield* in connection with Wakeman. Twain's final residence at Redding, Connecticut, was first named "Innocence at Home"; but Clara renamed it "Stormfield" because publication of the story by that name in *Harper's Magazine* paid for the loggia and the apartment over it; and Twain himself felt the name more appropriate.

In his *Autobiography* in 1906 Twain said the idea for the story came from Wakeman: "Captain Wakeman had a fine large imagination and he once told me of a visit which he had made to heaven. I kept it in my mind and a month or two later I put it on paper—this was in the first quarter of 1868, I think." In the *Autobiography,* however, Twain's memory was almost completely unreliable. The evidence in the Notebooks, written when his memory was much fresher, that Wakeman did not tell him the story is thoroughly convincing.

First, Twain's second trip with Wakeman, which was in March, did not occur early enough for him to have "kept" the recounting of the dream in "mind and a month or two later" put it "on paper" in "the first quarter of 1868," if that is his meaning in the entry in the *Autobiography*. Second, although Twain had written down immediately the material given him on the first trip with Wakeman, there is during and after this second trip no list, no entry, of such material; in fact, there is nothing in any of Twain's writings specifically pointing to this second trip with Wakeman. Although arguing from lack of evidence is hazardous, one is almost forced to conclude that Twain's second trip with Wakeman was different from the first—that Twain did not see so much of the Captain as he had earlier, that he was not so much impressed by the Captain, that he had other things to do, or, most probably, that he was not given any new supply of material from the Captain. If Twain had been told of such a marvelous dream, he would undoubtedly have recorded it in his Notebooks.

In the Notebooks that he was keeping during the first voyage with Wakeman in 1866 Twain carefully set down material that the Captain gave him. After the end of this voyage and while sailing up the Atlantic to New York Twain put down his remembered points:

Wakeman's Boat—Disengaging invention.
Capt. W's condors (full of epicures) that turn sheep inside out.

. . . .

Rats that left the sinking ship.
Do do do—and hauled up a sick comrade.

. . . .

Educated porpoises in Australia—tattooing and driving feathers in head to grow.
Hanging the Negro in the Chinchas.[18]

On the trip to the Holy Land later that year, made with the other "Innocents" on the *Quaker City*, Twain noted another anecdote that had been given to him by Wakeman. In none of these listings is there any hint or anything even remotely resembling the story of Stormfield's trip to heaven.

INTRODUCTION

In a later entry in the Notebooks (1887-88) there is another full account of the material Wakeman gave Twain:

Wakeman—Prophets of Baal & Isaac
" [sic]—Hanging the English Mate
"   —Courtship
"   —Daniel in Lion's den
"   —Stealing clipper ship
"   —Shipping as a boy with the saint [sic][19]

Further, about this time (1878) Twain wrote the long letter to his brother Orion already mentioned, in which he noted the beginning of his work on *Stormfield:* "(Eight) Nine years ago I mapped out my 'Journey in Heaven' [sic]. I discussed it with literary friends whom I could trust to keep it to themselves. I gave it a deal of thought, from time to time. After a year or more, I wrote it up. It was not a success. Five years ago I wrote it again, altering the plan."

With all these recollections of the Captain and with the itemizing of Wakeman material during the twenty years that Twain had been working on *Stormfield,* it is almost inconceivable that Twain would not have associated the origin with the Captain—if, indeed, the association was not the sheer fancy of his last years.

If Wakeman was not the source of the idea, where did Twain get it? The probable truth is arrived at by resolving some of Twain's contradictory statements. In an unpublished section of the Notebooks (#31 [II], Dec. 13, 1896-Jan. 6, 1897, p. 55) Twain made this entry: "What was her [Susy's] opinion of Capt. Stormfield's visit to Heaven (*Begun* in the winter of 1867-8 *as a (bur) satire* upon the 'Gates Ajar' & still in MS?" [my italics]. In the section of the *Autobiography* where Twain said that Wakeman had told him of the visit, he remarked that five or six years after writing the story he had showed it to William Dean Howells, who said, "Publish it." Twain continues: "I had turned it into a burlesque of 'The Gates Ajar'." Of the two comments the earlier one is probably more nearly accurate. It was written just after Susy's death, when Twain was tearing out his soul searching for consolation; the second comes at a time when Twain was dictating and when he often rambled on endlessly without much thought. This evidence that Twain began *Stormfield* as a direct answer to *Gates Ajar* is substantiated by a statement Twain made in 1907, in "Mental Telegraphy?" (published for the first time in this volume), which, although suspect because of its late date, can nevertheless be used as corroboration of stronger evidence: "I began the article (*Stormfield*) forty or forty-one years ago as a good-natured satire upon 'The Gates Ajar'...."

This novel, by Elizabeth Stuart Phelps, published in 1868, was a sentimental story about a New England girl who had lost her lover in the Civil War. Although it appealed to thousands of women who had experienced the same or a similar loss, it did not appeal to Twain. Exasperated by Miss Phelps's "mean little ten-cent heaven about the size of Rhode Island," as he recalled it in his *Autobiography* years later, he determined to enlarge the haven of good souls, to allow "ten per cent of the contents of the modern cemeteries; also as a volunteer kindness I let in a tenth of one per cent of the pagans who had died during the preceding eons." There is no doubt, therefore, that this saccharine novel was the origin, or one of the origins, of Twain's *Stormfield*.

But there is great likelihood that another item was strongly influential on the story, if not actually one of the origins, although Twain never mentions it by name: a cheap jokebook published in 1864 called *Old Abe's Jokes: Fresh from Abraham's Bosom. Containing all his issues, Excepting the 'Greenbacks.' To Call in some of which, this book is issued* (New York: T. R. Dawley). The wording of the subtitle is significant. The material in this book undoubtedly had been printed before, perhaps more than once; and it therefore was probably several years older than 1864 and known outside New York and off the Eastern seaboard.

Such inexpensive books—published by the hundreds and widespread—drew upon material in the popular mind and, in turn, re-popularized it. That Twain's mind would gravitate to this kind of humor goes without saying, for in his early days he was a prankster and liked rough humor. On the Virginia City *Enterprise* (1862-64) Twain hardened his literary muscles on such burlesques as "The Petrified Man" and "The Dutch Nick Massacre." In San Francisco after 1863 he associated with the group of Bohemians (including Bret Harte, Charles Henry Webb, and Ada Clara) who made it their business to write burlesque novels, the rage at that time. Twain himself wrote twenty-three burlesques and parodies.[20] After arriving in New York in 1867, Twain, as a reporter to Californians, frequented the theater and popular entertainments, where he surely heard this kind of humor. By 1878 he was being published in joke books[21] by Dick & Fitzgerald, the most famous such publisher; and in 1880-81 he was consulting these books for his proposed volume of American humor.

The anecdote in *Old Abe's Jokes*, which almost surely helped shape *Stormfield*, is entitled "Old Abe's 'Slap' at Chicago" (114-16). It is the story of a St. Louis man who went to Chicago and registered at a hotel. Since he was plainly dressed and seemed financially undistinguished, the proprietor of the hotel and his underlings paid little attention to him. Suddenly he was seized with illness and apparently died. In preparing the corpse for burial, the hotel people discovered that the man was in fact wealthy. Thereupon their attitude changed remarkably, and they became overly solicitous. The man awoke before burial, having been the victim of catalepsy. When someone asked how things had appeared to him while he was in the trance, the man replied that he had taken a trip to heaven. When he reached the Pearly Gate, he found St. Peter, "who opened the door at my summons, pipe in mouth, seated by a small table, on which stood a goodly mug of steaming whiskey toddy." St. Peter inquired where the man had lived. "St. Louis," he replied; and St. Peter was satisfied. "And where did you die?" St. Peter asked. When the man replied that he had died in Chicago, St. Peter protested. " 'Chicago?' said he, shaking his head, 'there's no such place, sir'." However, the man finally pointed it out on a "splendid atlas," and St. Peter concluded, " 'All right, sir,' said he after a moment's pause; 'it's there, sure enough, so walk in sir; but I'll be blest if you ain't the first man who ever came here from that place!' "

Such a story would certainly have appealed to Twain. Still a Missouri—and Western—man, he would have been pleased with the superiority of the St. Louis man over the Chicago people. In fact, Twain loved jokes about the hell-bound Chicagoans: in his Notebooks he entered this witticism at least twice—"Satan, to new-comer (with discontent). 'The trouble with you Chicago people is, that *you* think you are the best people in hell—where you're merely the most *numerous*.'"[22] Furthermore, this story would have appealed to Twain because it demonstrated man's venality, despite the fact that his own extreme pessimism was years in the future. The picture of St. Peter with pipe in mouth and toddy in hand is similar in tone to that of Twain's head clerk. But the greatest similarity between the two stories is the two incidents about whether or not the points of origin of the heaven-seekers—Chicago for the St. Louis man, Earth for Stormfield—really exist, and the consequent proof when a map is consulted.

Finally, there is an entry in Twain's Notebooks which, although enigmatical, is irrefutable proof that Twain knew either the anecdote or one like it. Between February 26 and September 8, 1879, Twain made a series of entries on three pages which seem to be random thoughts, some new, some remembered and old, having been put down in the Notebooks numerous times before. It is, therefore, impossible to determine whether any particular item is newly learned or merely recollected:

> St. Peter "You're the first man ever came here from Chicago."
> Devil (When Potter threw?)—Come, play fair, none of your miracles—Organize!
> Drunk man—Is that the moon? 2d DM—Don't know—I don't live around here.
>
> . . . .
>
> "Adam? What's his other name?"
> Isaac & Prophets of Baal
> Wakeman first sees his wife[23]

The first entry is unquestionably from "Old Abe's 'Slap' at Chicago" or something like it. The others are pretty surely jokebook or minstrel humor, and some refer to two anecdotes Wakeman had given him long before. Part of the enigma of these entries is that at this time Twain had been a year and a half in Europe and almost surely would not have had access to these ephemeral jokebooks. This plethora of such humor may indicate that he had just sat in on a feast of joke telling. But the likelier explanation is probably that, for one reason or another, he was merely recording remembered items, as he frequently did. For example, the Adam line, third from the bottom above, occurs in the Notebooks some eight years later all alone and with no context or reference: "Adam? What was his first name?"[24]

Indeed, in the light of the mixture of entries given above, Twain's attributing the origin of the dream about Stormfield to Wakeman may in fact be a kind of proof that he derived it from a popular source.

III

The history of the manuscripts of the story reveals a saga of noble intentions but weak execution. Having got the *ideas,* as Twain called them, in 1868 or before, he forever searched for the plans of development, as he wrote to Orion, in the letter mentioned above: "Mind, I never have altered the ideas, from the first—the *plan* was the difficulty." The earliest extant manuscript is one on which is penciled —probably by A. B. Paine, Twain's biographer—the date 1868. It was written mostly on Crystal Lake Mills stationery. The ink used at the beginning is dark red; that used later is black. This version may have been Twain's earliest effort. But it runs to one hundred and fifteen pages, and it generally corresponds to the version printed in Dixon Wecter's *Report from Paradise.* It probably dates, as Wecter conjectured, from the 1870's.[25]

The fullest manuscript version is now among the Mark Twain Papers at Berkeley, California, including the two chapters never before published and included in this volume. One of these two, entitled "Captain Stormfield Resumes," has on it Paine's notation, "Not of much literary value? [sic]". It was omitted from De Voto's *Mark Twain in Eruption* because it was, in De Voto's mind, "mediocre." Wecter called both sections "too scrappy or uninspired to be worth salvage," and they were therefore excluded from the "full" version he published in *Report from Paradise.* Both De Voto's and Wecter's value judgments are open to question: neither of these two chapters is quite so good as the better portions of the other sections, but neither is contemptible. Both are therefore included in this volume.

There are, furthermore, in the Notebooks numerous notes Twain wrote to himself on various ways the story was to be continued and broadened. Some are full-blown; some, mere half-thoughts. In this volume I have included all of them in footnotes because they are extremely important in chronicling the course of Twain's thinking on this subject through the years and in revealing the literary development of the subject that was probably his greatest obsession —his fight with Heaven.

INTRODUCTION

The version given in this volume is, therefore, as nearly as possible the "complete" text. But regrettably it does not include all versions because one—at least—is now lost. Wecter described this lost manuscript as "an eleven-page passage, which Mark finally jettisoned from the printed version." In it, according to Wecter, Twain "went more fully into a topic broached at the start of Chapter IV, the Captain's awkward attempts to fly. Again and again the wind upsets his reckonings, landing him a-sprawl in the briers. Reasoning that birds handle their wings better because they have a rudder, the Captain plucks out a fistful of feathers and fastens them on behind." Then Wecter quotes a short passage:

> They were not a part of me, and I couldn't work them, they only just stuck out behind in a foolish bunch like a feather-duster and didn't do any good. And then some boys came along and one of them said,—
> "Oh, here's fun! Here's an angel with a tail. Let's clod him."
> They did clod me, too, and I had to fly into some woods a mile off to get away from them.

Wecter concludes his resume: "In disgust, he says, 'I rolled up my wings in an old last week's *Zion Herald,* and tucked them away in the pantry'."[26]

Twain's reluctance through the years to publish the story might have stemmed from Livy's desire not to shock the sensibilities of religious people, although she personally had long since come to her husband's persuasion that there is no personal God. Paine says the manuscript "lay under the ban" for years, presumably Livy's. No doubt another reason was its unfinished state. But clearly Twain himself felt the treatment of the subject potentially explosive, or he would not have set a time fuse for fifty years in the future by planning to consign the manuscript to the *Autobiography,* which was to be published only after half a century. The truth is, however, that today the story is mild satire and pale agnosticism and was so in fact by the turn of the century. Twain's dragon of forty years before was by 1909 spewing Seltzer water. Mark's squeamishness demonstrates how fully he was a child of the nineteenth century.[27]

IV

The clerical self-importance that Twain so despised formed the core of another story that he long cherished, "The Late Reverend Sam Jones's Reception in Heaven," also published in this volume for the first time. Written while Twain was in Germany in the winter of 1891-92, it too lay under the ban of both Livy and Mark. In a penciled notation at the top of the manuscript are Twain's words, "Not published—forbidden by Mrs. Clemens, S.L.C." As he said later, in the article on George Bernard Shaw and mental telepathy also included in this volume, "I was ever so fond of that 'Reception' article, and dearly wanted to print it, but it was hilarious and extravagant to the very verge of impropriety, and I could not beguile my wife into consenting to its publication." But in these statements Twain was—typically—shifting to Livy's shoulders reservations he also felt. When Twain translated the story into German, Paine said that Twain's idea was to publish it surreptitiously; "but," in Paine's words, "his conscience had been too much for him." Twain had confessed to his wife, and even the German version had been suppressed.

The object of satire in this brief story is the Reverend Samuel Porter Jones, commonly known as Sam Jones, who was admitted to the Georgia bar in 1869 but whose career in the law ended because of his drinking. He was converted in 1872 and, probably because of his eccentricities of speech and manner, became popular as an evangelist. To Twain, Jones was "sweeping the South like a cyclone with his revival meetings, and converting the unconverted here and there and everywhere with his thundering torrents of piety and slang." In this story, Twain's own dream, Mark is on a train bound for the hereafter with the Reverend Jones and the Archbishop of Canterbury. Twain, not ticketed for heaven because he is a humorist, switches cards with the Archbishop, gets off the train with Glory-bound Jones, witnesses his reception by the Elect, and the chaos that ensues. The story reflects again Twain's respect for the aphorism, "Heaven for climate; hell for society."

After writing this story, Twain closely associated it with its blood brother, *Stormfield*. In the Notebooks both are frequently mentioned together. When, for example, Twain was brooding after Susy's death over what she had thought about the earlier story, he wondered also how she had evaluated the later one. Although the story is short and narrow in purpose, one is likely to rate it high among Twain's lesser accomplishments. It is altogether fitting that these two stories be published together in this volume. And it is appropriate also that the third item in this collection, the hitherto-unpublished sketch on "Mental Telegraphy?" (Twain's own word), should be included; for it throws light on the two short stories and reveals another facet of Twain's ever-abiding interest in telepathy.

V

The material in this volume, in addition to being good reading, is significant for two reasons. First, although Twain's argument with heaven, with conventional religion, and the usual concept of the hereafter has been known in outline, this material gives certain shadings indispensable to anyone genuinely interested in this aspect of Twain. Secondly, here is presented in the *Stormfield* material the growth of an idea, the development of a literary work, its planning, its viable and still-born ideas, its stumblings as well as its firm steps forward. As such, it is an informative revelation about Twain the literary artist and the man.

References to Introduction

1. Unless otherwise stated, all references to the Mark Twain Papers (hereafter MTP) are to those in the General Library, University of California, Berkeley. For this quotation see Notebook #29 (II), April 8, 1896-April 28, 1896, p. 45. Copyright the Mark Twain Company 1970.

2. A. B. Paine, *Mark Twain, A Biography* (New York: Harper & Brothers, 1929), IV, 1482.

3. MTP. Notebook #35, 1902, p. 23. Yet only a few years earlier Twain was writing, in Notebook #32b (II), Sept. 24, 1897-Aug. 18, 1899, p. 63: "There has been only one Christian. They caught and crucified him—early." Copyright the Mark Twain Company 1970.

4. MTP. Notebook #32 (I), Jan. 7, 1892-Aug. 23, 1899, p. 12. Copyright the Mark Twain Company 1970.

5. MTP. Notebook #32b (II), Sept. 24, 1897-Aug. 18, 1899, p. 63. Copyright the Mark Twain Company 1970.

6. MTP. Notebook #38, 1905-08, p. 5. The full quotation about the fly is, "The morals of a God ought to be minutely perfect. I would not worship a God that made the fly" (Notebook #36, 1903, p. 11). Five pages later he continued his quirk of character with another statement: "If God invented the fly, that is enough. It gives us the measure of His character. If a man invented the fly, we should curse him forever. And he would deserve it" (*Ibid.*, p. 16). Both items copyright the Mark Twain Company 1970.

7. MTP. Notebook #30 (II), June 1, 1896-July 16, 1896, pp. 52-53. Copyright the Mark Twain Company 1970.

8. MTP. Notebook #32 (I), Jan. 7, 1897-Aug. 23, 1898, p. 19, and Notebook #36, 1903, p. 10; an abbreviated version—"Heaven for climate"—was entered in Notebook #34, 1901, p. 16. The Philadelphia reference is in Notebook #32 (II), Dec. 13, 1896-Jan. 6, 1897, p. 39, plus another immediately following: "The materialized spirit said (but this was years and years and years ago) that the only resemblance *he* could see between hell and Philadelphia was that both were paved with the same material." The Ingersoll item is in Note-

REFERENCES TO INTRODUCTION

book #28 (I), March 6, 1895-Dec. 13, 1895, p. 6. Copyright the Mark Twain Company 1970.

9. For the full letter see A. B. Paine, *Mark Twain's Letters* (New York: Harper & Brothers, 1929), I, 322-25.

10. "Let us (smoke) swear while we may, for in heaven it will not be allowed." "If I cannot swear in Heaven I shall not stay there." Notebook #32b (II), Sept. 24, 1897-Aug. 18, 1899, p. 64. Copyright the Mark Twain Company 1970.

11. A manuscript owned by the American Academy of Arts and Letters, given them by A. B. Paine, has a title page in the hand of Paine:

>   Travels of Capt. Eli Stormfield, Mariner in Heaven,
>   Taken down from his own Lips by
>   Rev. George H. Peters, of Marysville, Calif.

In "Rambling Notes" Twain has an anecdote about Captain Hurricane Jones which gives Twichell the name "The Rev. Mr. Peters."

12. MTP. Notebook #36, 1903, p. 14.

13. MTP. Notebook #32a (II), June 2, 1897-July 24, 1897, pp. 54-55.

14. Quoted in Dixon Wecter, ed., *Report from Paradise* (New York: Harper & Brothers, 1952), p. xxii: also in Paine's biography, p. 840.

15. Quoted in Bernard De Voto, ed., *Mark Twain in Eruption* (New York: Grosset & Dunlap, 1940), p. 248.

16. MTP. *Autobiography*, Typescript, August 30, 1906. Copyright the Mark Twain Company 1970.

17. Several still-born items in the Notebooks are interesting. In one which merely refers to an "event," there is a listing of names of persons who obviously are staffing a ship: Orion, Twain's brother, is listed as second mate; Wakeman as chief mate (Notebook #32a (I), Jan. 7, 1897-June 15, 1897, p. 26); and another is:

>   Captain, our meek Arundel and his trifling officers. Scotch Captain afterwards picked up—old Ned Wakeman American [sic]. (Stormfield) (take the kindliness out of him—make him hard, and a scoffer at religion.) Been a pirate and slaver 40 years before, 1815 to '30. Born at sea. Stole a ship once. Accosted on fo'castle: 'who are *you?*' 'The storekeeper.'
>
>   To a Cal desperado who had terrorized the ship all across the Pacific —in a low sweet voice: 'Did you hear me say you must not threaten anybody in this ship?'

[33]

'Well, sir, and suppose—' hit on jaw with palm and sent sprawling. When he gets up: 'Go to forecastle—and stay there the voyage.'

Afterward, in the Race, this man murders somebody and flies to a ship where some mutineers have taken refuge. Wakeman steals over in the night, a week later, and marches to fo'castle with his gun over shoulder of a dear friend of the desperado, and captures him, fetches him back, and next morning hangs him. (Notebook #31b (I), June 22, 1897-Sept. 24, 1897, p. 31f.)

Another interesting entry is this one:

In the S[andwich] I[sland] story, make old Commodore (smith) cyclone a frequent and red-hot letter writer, whose whirlwinds of temper are gone by the time the letter is finished. The letter reeks with blasphemy and earthrocking profanity. But now (?) he strikes dimly out, interlines, and the letter is as mild as a sucking dove. Always put in and strikes out, as in Holmes's temperance song.

(Notebook #17 May 1883-Aug. 12, 1884, p. 33). Obviously, Wakeman was the original of that portrait. Both items copyright the Mark Twain Company 1970.

"The Great Dark," in John S. Tuckey, ed., *Which Was the Dream? and Other Symbolic Writings of the Later Years* (Berkeley: Univ. of Calif. Press, 1967) has a brief passage exactly paralleling in tone and phraseology the section in *Stormfield*, Chapter I, beginning with "'Eight Bells, sir.' 'Make it so'." Also there is a suggestive entry in the Notebooks for November 4, 1893: "Si Wheeler's arrival in Heaven." Wheeler, hero of Twain's abortive play, *Simon Wheeler, the Amateur Detective*, is the storyteller of "The Celebrated Jumping Frog of Calaveras County." Was Twain thinking of getting more captains, or visitors, into Heaven? It hardly seems likely that he was going to displace Wakeman. For a full study of the Twain-Wakeman friendship see, Ray B. Browne, "Mark Twain and Captain Wakeman," *American Literature*, XXXIII (Nov., 1961), 320-29.

18. MTP. Notebook #6, Nov. 15, 1866-Jan. 12, 1867, p. 8. Copyright the Mark Twain Company 1970.

19. MTP. Notebook #22 (II), Nov. 1887-June 1888, p. 43. Copyright the Mark Twain Company 1970.

20. For a good study of this subject see Franklin R. Rogers, *Mark Twain's Burlesque Patterns* (Dallas, Texas: Southern Methodist University Press, 1960).

21. Twain was especially interested in the San Francisco Minstrels, one of the great minstrel groups, that had left the Bay City for New

REFERENCES TO INTRODUCTION

York about 1864. Out of delight as well as duty, Twain saw their performance, as he wrote, "pretty often." This group, whom he calls in *Roughing It* the "showmen," had taken over his catchy announcement in San Francisco: "The trouble will begin at 8 o'clock." Through use in the Minstrels' advertisements, the statement had been spread everywhere; Twain even found it scribbled on the wall of a jail cell in New York. A minstrel variant was the title of a skit named "De trouble begins at nine: Deeds of Darkness."

But Twain provided longer copy for the popular stage, as the following extract of Negro minstrelsy reveals. Entitled "The Jumping Frog," the section consists of repartee between the End Man and the Middle Man. The former leads up to his crescendo by relating that in a hotel he once found his bed so filled with bed bugs that he called the landlord and asked for a set of harness; he was going to take a ride in his bed because it had become a "little buggy." Then the following dialogue ensues:

Middle Man—What did he do?

End Man —He went and stood the segars.

MM —A very good fellow.

EM —No. He played an awful mean trick on me. I had a little frog that I had trained to jump. He was the best jumper you ever saw. I was telling the landlord about him and I told him I'd bet twenty-five dollars that my frog could outjump any frog in the country. He took the bet, and he says, go down to the frog pond and get me a frog.

MM —Did you?

EM —Yes. I thought I would accommodate him. I knew I had a sure thing. I knew my frog could hop the life out of any other, so I went down to the frog pond and caught a big one and came back. We put the two frogs side by side. I says, When we say "ready" you touch your frog and I'll touch mine—whichever jumps the farthest takes the money. So we said "ready." He touched his frog and I touched mine.

MM —What was the result?

EM —His frog jumped clean over into the pond. Mine didn't budge an inch. Didn't move!

MM —Why, how was that?

EM —Well, you see when I went to catch a frog for the landlord, he made my frog swallow a handful of buckshot, and it loaded him so heavy that he couldn't move.

From Frank Dumont, *Burnt Cork: or, The Amateur Minstrel* (New York: Dick & Fitzgerald), p. 67.

22. MTP. Notebook #32a (I), Jan. 7, 1897-June 15, 1897, p. 12; #32b (II), Sept. 24, 1897-Aug. 1899, p. 72. Copyright the Mark Twain Company 1970.

23. MTP. Notebook #14, Feb. 26, 1879-Sept. 8, 1879, pp. 48-50. Copyright the Mark Twain Company 1970.

24. MTP. Notebook #22 (II), Nov. 1887-June, 1888, p. 57. Copyright the Mark Twain Company 1970.

25. At the end of Chapter Two of this manuscript (Chapter Four in the present volume) there is an interesting notation in pencil, probably by A. B. Paine, which reads:

> Map of Section No. 4,785,696 of Heaven—showing position of our world—also smallness of our world as compared with that division of heaven. A map of *all* heaven, drawn to this scale, would stretch in all directions farther than any star visible through the most powerful telescope is removed from us—say 500000000000 miles long & wide.
>
> A school map of our own system would be *12 miles long,* to include Neptune & Uranus, so Proctor says.
>
> The Wart—enlarged slightly beyond its just size, to enable it to be seen with the naked eye.

26. Surely the most curious of the *Stormfield* manuscripts is owned by the American Academy of Arts and Letters, entitled "Captain Wakeman's Travels in Heaven," with the subtitle "Visit to Spiritual Dept and impalpable bodies." It bears the date 1877 in pencil on the first page, possibly in a hand other than Twain's; and it consists of an autobiographical sketch of a boyhood in Missouri along with a kind of inventory of commodities and their prices.

27. The heaven that Twain creates and hopes for is quite different from Talmage's expectations. But Mark's uncertainty about what the next world would really be like is revealed in his unpublished review of *The Cities of the Sun* (1901), a book by a fellow-Missourian, George Woodward Warder. Twain commented: "Any book which can increase our knowledge of our final home should be welcome." Then he touched on topics which he had already discussed in *Stormfield:*

> Mr. Warder has opened my eyes to the mighty dimensions of the New Jerusalem, and for this service I am his obliged debtor.... I suddenly see the little New Jerusalem expand and cover a continent, and lift its soaring masses skyward up and up, hundreds of miles, and fade twinkling out in remoteness beyond the reach of human vision!...

REFERENCES TO INTRODUCTION

It makes one's mouth water. It would be a wonderful experience to stand there in those enchanted surroundings and hear Shakespeare and Milton and Bunyan read from their noble works. And it might be that they would like to hear me read some of my things. No, it could never be; they would not care for me. They would not know me, they would not understand me, and they would say they had an engagement. But if I could only be there, and walk about and look, and listen, I should be satisfied and not make a noise. My life is fading to its close, and someday I shall know. (Copyright the Mark Twain Company 1970)

PART ONE

Captain Stormfield's Visit to Heaven

Note. I knew Captain Stormfield well. I made three long sea-voyages with him in his ship. He was a rugged, weather-tanned sailor, with a picked-up education, a sterling good heart, an iron will, abundant pluck, unshakable beliefs and convictions, and a confidence in himself which had no discoverable limits. He was open, frank, communicative, affectionate, and as honest, simple and genuine as a dog. He was deeply religious, by nature and by the training of his mother, and a fluent and desolating swearer by the training of his father and by the necessities of his occupation. He was born in his father's ship, he had spent his entire life at sea, and had seen the edges of all lands and the interiors of none, and when I first knew him he was sixty-five years old and his glossy black hair and whiskers were beginning to show threads of gray; but there was no trace of age in his body, yet, nor in his determined spirit, and the fires that burned in his eyes were the fires of youth. He was a lovable man when people pleased him, but a tough person to deal with when the case was otherwise.

He had a good deal of imagination, and it probably colored his statements of fact; but if this was so, he was not aware of it. He made no statement which he did not believe to be true. When he told me about his strange and uncanny adventures in the Devil's Race-Track—a vast area in the solitudes of the South Pacific where the needle of the compass is powerless to exercise its office and whizzes madly and continuously around—I spared him the hurt of suggesting that he had dreamed the tale, for I saw that he was in earnest; but in secret I believed it was only a vision, a dream. Privately I think his visit to the Other World was a dream, also, but I did not wound him with the expression of the thought. He believed that the visit was an actual experience; I accepted it on those terms, listened to it attentively, took down the details of each day's revelations in short-hand, by his permission, then afterward reduced the result to long-hand. I have polished some of the ruggedness out of his grammar and construction, and in places I have cooled off his language a little; otherwise his tale stands here as he told it.

MARK TWAIN

CHAPTER I

I WAS DYING, and knew it. I was making gasps, with long spaces between, and they were standing around the bed, quiet and still, waiting for me to go. Now and then they spoke; and what they said got dimmer and dimmer, and further and further away. I heard it all, though. The mate said—
"He's going out with the tide."
Chips the carpenter said—
"How do you know? No tide out here in the middle of the ocean."
"Yes there is. And anyway, they always do."
It was still again, a while—only the heaving and creaking, and the dull lanterns swinging this way and that, and the wind wheezing and piping, far off. Then I heard a voice, away off—
"Eight bells, sir."
"Make it so," said the mate.
"Ay-ay, sir."
Another voice—
"Freshening up, sir—coming on to blow."
"Sheet home," says the mate. "Reef tops'ls and sky-scrapers, and stand by."
"Ay-ay, sir."
By and by the mate says—
"How's it now?"
"He's cold, up to his ribs," says the doctor. "Give him ten minutes."
"Everything ready, Chips?"
"Canvas, cannon balls and all, sir."
"Bible and burial service?"
"All handy, sir."

Quiet again, for a while—wind so vague it sounded like dream-wind. Then the doctor's voice—

"Is he prepared for the change, do you think?"

"To hell? Oh, I guess so."

"I reckon there ain't any doubt."

It was Chips said it; kind of mournful, too.

"Doubt?" said the mate. "Hadn't any himself, if that's any sign."

"No," says Chips, "he always said he judged he was booked for there."

Long, long stillness. Then the doctor's voice, so far off and dim it sounded like it was down a deep well—

"There—it's over! Just at 12:14!"

Dark? Oh, pitch dark—all in a second! I was dead, and knew it.

I felt myself make a plunge, and recognized that I was flashing through the air like a bird. I had a quick, dim glimpse of the sea and the ship, then everything was black darkness, and nothing visible, and I went whizzing through it. I said to myself, "I'm all here, clothes and all, nothing missing; they'll sink a counterfeit in the sea; it's not me, I'm all here."

Next, it began to get light, and straight off I plunged into a whole universe of blinding fire, and straight through it. It was 12:22 by my watch.

Do you know where I was? In the sun. That was my guess, and it turned out afterwards that I was right. Eight minutes out from port. It gave me my gait—exactly the speed of light, 186,000 miles a second. Ninety-three million miles in eight minutes by the watch. There wasn't ever a prouder ghost. I was as pleased as a child, and wished I had something to race with.

Before I was done thinking these things I was out on the other side and the sun shriveling up to a luminous wad behind me. It was less than a million miles in diameter, and I was through before I had time to get warm. I was in the dark again, now. In the dark; but I myself wasn't dark. My body gave out a soft and ghostly glow and I felt like a lightning bug. I couldn't make out the why of this, but I could read my watch by it, and that was more to the point.

Presently I noticed a glow like my own a little way off, and was glad, and made a trumpet of my hands and hailed it—

"Shipmate ahoy!"
"Same to you!"
"Where from?"
"Chatham Street."
"Whither bound?"
"I vish I knew—aind it?"
"I reckon you're going my way. Name?"
"Solomon Goldstein. Yours?"
"Captain Ben Stormfield, late of Fairhaven and 'Frisco. Come alongside, friend."

He did it. It was a great improvement, having company. I was born sociable, and never could stand solitude. I was trained to a prejudice against Jews—Christians always are, you know—but such of it as I had was in my head, there wasn't any in my heart. But if I had been full of it it would have disappeared then, I was so lonesome and so anxious for company. Dear me, when you are going to—to—where I was going—you are humble-minder than you used to be, and thankful for whatever you can get, never mind the quality of it.

We spun along together, and talked, and got acquainted and had a good time. I thought it would be a kindness to Solomon to dissipate his doubts, so that he would have a quiet mind. I could never be comfortable in a state of doubt myself. So I reasoned the thing out, and showed him that his being pointed the same as me was proof of where he was bound for. It cost him a good deal of distress, but in the end he was reconciled and said it was probably best the way it was, he wouldn't be suitable company for angels and they would turn him down if he tried to work in; he had been treated like that in New York, and he judged that the ways of high society were about the same everywhere. He wanted me not to desert him when we got to where we were going, but stay by him, for he would be a stranger and friendless. Poor fellow, I was touched; and promised—"to all eternity."

Then we were quiet a long time, and I let him alone, and let him think. It would do him good. Now and then he sighed, and by and by I found he was crying. You know, I was mad with him in a minute; and says to myself, "Just like a Jew! he has promised some hayseed or other a coat for four dollars, and now he has made up his mind that if he was back he could work off a worse one on him for five. They haven't any heart—that race—nor any principles."

He sobbed along to himself, and I got colder and colder and harder and harder towards him. At last I broke out and said—

"Cheese it! Damn the coat! Drop it out of your mind."

"Goat?"

"Yes. Find something else to cry about."

"Why, I wasn't crying apoud a goat."

"What then?"

"Oh, captain. I lost my little taughter, and now I never, never see her again any more. It break my heart!"

By God, it went through me like a knife! I wouldn't feel so mean again, and so grieved, not for a fleet of ships. And I spoke out and said what I felt; and went on damning myself for a hound till he was so distressed I had to stop; but I wasn't half through. He begged me not to talk so, and said I oughtn't to make so much of what I had done; he said it was only a mistake, and a mistake wasn't a crime.

There now—wasn't it magnanimous? I ask you—wasn't it? I think so. To my mind there was the stuff in him for a Christian; and I came out flat-footed and told him so. And if it hadn't been too late I would have reformed him and made him one, or died in the act.

We were good friends again, and he didn't need to keep his sorrows to himself any more, he could pour them right into my heart, which was wide open and ready; and he did; till it seemed to me I couldn't bear it. Lord, the misery of it! She was his pet, his playfellow, the apple of his eye; she was ten years old, and dead six months, and he was glad to die, himself, so he could have her in his arms again and be with her always—and now that dream was over. Why, she was gone—*forever*. The word had a new meaning. It took my breath, it made me gasp. All our lives we believe we are going to see our lost friends again—we are not disturbed with doubts, we think we *know* it. It is what keeps us alive. And here, in this father's heart that hope was dead. I had never seen that before. This was the first time, and I—why it was I that had killed it. If I had only thought! If I had only kept still, and left him to find it out for himself. He let his tears run, and now and then his trouble wrung a groan out of him, and his lips quivered and he said—

"Poor little Minnie—and poor me."

And to myself I said the same—

"Poor little Minnie—and poor me."

That feeling stayed by me, and never left me. And many's the time, when I was thinking of that poor Jew's disaster, I have said in my thoughts, "I wish I was bound for heaven, and could trade places with him, so he could see his child, damned if I wouldn't do it." If ever you are situated like that, you will understand the feeling.

CHAPTER II

WE TALKED LATE, and fell asleep pretty tired, about two in the morning; had a sound sleep, and woke refreshed and fine towards noon. Pitch dark, still. We were not hungry, but I could have smoked with a relish, if I had had the things. Also, I could have enjoyed a drink.

We had to stop and think a minute, when we woke, before we came fully to ourselves and realized our situation, for we thought we had been dreaming. In fact it was hard to get rid of the idea that it was all a dream. But we had to get rid of it, and we did. Then a ghastly cold shock went through us—we remembered where we were pointed for. Next, we were astonished. Astonished because we hadn't arrived. Astonished and glad. Glad we hadn't arrived. Hopeful that we might not arrive for some little time yet.

"How far is it that ve haf come, Captain Sthormfilt?"

"Eleven or twelve hundred million miles."

"Ach Gott, it is a speed!"

"Right you are. There isn't anything that can pass us but thought. It would take the lightning express twenty-four or twenty-five days to fly around the globe; we could do it four times in a second—yes, sir, and do it easy. Solomon, I wish we had something to race with."

Along in the afternoon we saw a soft blur of light a little way off, north-east-by-east-half-east, about two points off the weather bow, and hailed it. It closed up on us, and turned out to be a corpse by the name of Bailey, from Oshkosh, that had died at 7:10 the night before. A good creature, but moony and reflective. Republican in politics, and had the idea that nothing could save civilization but that party. He was melancholy, and we got him to talk, so as to cheer him up; and along by spells, as he got to feeling better, his private matters got to leaking out—among others, the fact that he had committed suicide. You know, we had suspected it; he had a hole through his forehead that you couldn't have plugged with a marlinespike.

By and by his spirits sagged again. Then the cause came out. He was delicate and sensitive in his morals, and he had been doing something in politics, the last thing, which he was wondering if it was exactly straight. There was an election to fill a vacancy in his town government, and it was such a close fit that one vote would decide it. He wasn't going to be there to vote—he was going to be up here, with us. But if he could keep a democrat from voting, that would answer just as well, and the republican candidate would pull through. So, when he was ready for suicide he went to a rigidly honorable friend, who was a democrat, and got him to pair off with him. The republican ticket was safe, then, and he killed himself. So he was a little troubled about it, and uncertain; afraid that maybe he hadn't played quite fair, for a Presbyterian.

But Solomon admired him, and thought it was an amazingly smart idea, and just gloated over him with envy, and grinned that Jew grin of intense satisfaction, you know, and slapped his thigh and said—

"Py Chorge, Pailey, almost thou persuadest me to pe a Ghristian."

It was about his girl that he killed himself—Candace Miller. He couldn't ever quite get her to say she loved him, though she seemed to, and he had good hopes. But the thing that decided him was a note from her, in which she told him she loved him as a friend, and hoped they would always be friends, but she found her heart belonged to another. Poor Bailey, he broke down there and cried.

Curious! Just then we sighted a blue light a little astern, and hailed it, and when it ranged up alongside Bailey shouted—

"Why Tom Wilson! what a happy surprise; what ever brought you here, comrade?"

Wilson gave him an appealing look that was sort of heartbreaking to see, and said—

"Don't welcome me like that, George, I'm not worthy. I'm a low-down dog, and not fit for any clean man's company."

"Don't!" said Bailey. "Don't talk like that. What is it?"

"George, I did a treacherous thing. To think I could do it to an old playfellow like you, that I was born and raised with! But it was only a silly practical joke, and I never dreamed that any harm could come of it. *I* wrote that letter. She loved you, George."

"My God!"

"Yes, she did. She was the first one to the house; and when she saw you lying dead in your blood and the letter by you, signed with her name, she read it and knew! She flung herself on your corpse, and kissed your face and your eyes, and poured out her love and her grief and despair, and I saw it. I had murdered you, I had broken her heart, I couldn't bear it—and I am here."

Another suicide, you see. Bailey—well, he couldn't go back, you know, and it was pitiful to see him, he was so frantic over what he had lost by killing himself before ever stopping to find out whether she wrote the letter or not. He kept on regretting and lamenting and wishing he had waited and been more rational, and arranging over and over again in different ways, how he ought to have acted, and how he would act now, if he could only have the chance over again. All no good, of course, and made us miserable to hear it, for he couldn't ever have his chance again forever—we realized that, and the whole ghastliness of the situation. Some people think you are at rest when you die. Let them wait, they'll see.

Solomon took Bailey aside to comfort him—a good idea; people that carry griefs in their hearts know how to comfort others' griefs.

We whizzed along about a week before we picked up

another straggler. This time it was a nigger. He was about thirty-eight or forty, and had been a slave nearly half of his life. Named Sam. A cheerful, good-natured cuss, and likeable. As I learned later, a pick-up is a depressing influence upon the company for some time, because he is full of thinkings about his people at home and their grief over losing him; and so his talk is all about that, and he wants sympathy, and cries a good deal, and tells you how dear and good his wife was, or his poor old mother, or his sisters and brothers, and of course in common kindness you have to listen, and it keeps the company feeling desolate and wretched for days together, and starts up their own sorrows over their own loss of family and friends; but when the pick-up is a young person that has lost a sweetheart, that is the worst. There isn't any end to their talk, and their sorrow and their tears. And dear, dear, that one tiresome everlasting question that they keep on asking till you are worn to the bone with it: *don't* we think he (or she) will die soon, and come? What can you say? There's only one thing: *yes*, we hope he will. And when you have said it a couple of thousand times, you lose patience and wish you hadn't died. But dead people are people, just the same, and they bring their habits with them, which is natural. On the earth, when you arrive in a city—any city on the globe—the people peck at you with the same old regular questions—

"First time you have visited our city?"

"How does it impress you?"

"When did you arrive?"

"How long are you going to stay?"

Sometimes you have to leave next day, to get a rest. We arranged differently with the lovers, by and by: we bunched them together to themselves and made them burn their own smoke. And it was no harm; they like it best that way. There was plenty of sympathy and sentiment, and that was what they wanted.

Sam had pipe, tobacco and matches; I cannot tell you how

glad I was. But only for a little moment; then there was a sharp disappointment: the matches wouldn't light. Bailey explained it: there was no atmosphere there in space, and the match couldn't burn without oxygen. I said we would keep the things—we might strike through the atmosphere of a planet or a sun, some time or other, and if it was a big one we might have time for one whiff, anyway. But he said no, it wasn't on the cards.

"Ours are spiritualized bodies and spiritualized clothes and things," he said, "otherwise they would have been consumed in a flash when we first darted through the earth's atmosphere. This is spiritualized tobacco, and fire-proof."

It was very annoying. But I said we would keep it, just the same—

"It will burn in hell, anyway."

When the nigger found that that was where I was going, it filled him with distress, and he hoped I was mistaken, and did his best to persuade me I was; but I hadn't any doubts, and so he had to give in. He was as grieved about it as my best friend could be, and tried his best to believe it wouldn't be as hot there as people said, and hoped and believed I would get used to it after a while, and not mind it. His kindly talk won me completely; and when he gave me the pipe and tobacco, and begged me to think of him sometimes when I was smoking, I was a good deal moved. He was a good chap, and like his race: I have seen but few niggers that hadn't their hearts in the right place.

As week after week slipped along by we picked up a straggler at intervals, and at the end of the first year our herd numbered 36. It looked like a flock of glow-worms, and was a quite pretty sight. We could have had a regiment if we had kept all we came across, but the speeds were various and that was an interference. The slowest ship makes the pace for the fleet, of course. I raised our gait a little, as an accommodation, and established it at 200,000 miles a second. Some wanted to get on faster, on account of wanting to join lost friends, so we let them go. I was not in a particular hurry, myself—my business would keep. Some that had been consumptives and such like, were rickety and slow, and they dropped behind and disappeared. Some that were troublesome and disagreeable, and always raising Cain over any little thing that didn't suit them, I ordered off the course, with a competent cursing and a warning to stand clear. We had all sorts left, young and old, and on the whole they were satisfactory enough, though a few of them were not up to standard, I will admit.

CHAPTER III

WELL, WHEN I HAD BEEN DEAD about thirty years, I begun to get a little anxious. Mind you, I had been whizzing through space all that time, like a comet. *Like* a comet! Why, Peters, I laid over the lot of them! Of course there warn't any of them going my way, as a steady thing, you know, because they travel in a long circle like the loop of a lasso, whereas I was pointed as straight as a dart for the Hereafter; but I happened on one every now and then that was going my way for an hour or so, and then we had a bit of a brush together. But it was generally pretty one-sided, because I sailed by them the same as if they were standing still. An ordinary comet don't make more than about 200,-000 miles a minute. Of course when I came across one of that sort—like Encke's and Halley's comets, for instance— it warn't anything but just a flash and a vanish, you see. You couldn't rightly call it a race. It was as if the comet was a gravel-train and I was a telegraph despatch. But after I got outside of our astronomical system, I used to flush a comet occasionally that was something *like*. *We* haven't got any such comets—ours don't begin. One night I was swinging along at a good round gait, everything taut and trim, and the wind in my favor—I judged I was going about a million miles a minute—it might have been more, it couldn't have been less—when I flushed a most uncommonly big one about three points off my starboard bow. By his stern lights I judged he was bearing about northeast-and-by-north-half-east. Well, it was so near my course that I wouldn't throw away the chance; so I fell off a point, steadied my helm, and went for him. You should have heard me whiz, and seen the electric fur fly! In about a minute and a half I was fringed out with an electrical nimbus that flamed around for miles and miles and lit up all space like broad day. The comet was burning blue in the distance, like a sickly torch, when I first sighted him, but he begun to grow bigger and bigger as I crept up on him. I slipped up on him so fast that when I had gone about 150,000,000 miles I was close enough to be swallowed up in the phosphorescent glory of his wake, and I couldn't see anything for the glare. Thinks I, it won't do to run into him, so I shunted to one side and tore along. By and by I closed up abreast of his tail. Do you know what it was like? It was like a gnat closing up on the continent of America. I forged along. By and by I had sailed along his coast for a little upwards of a hundred and fifty million miles, and then I could see by the shape of him that I hadn't even got up to his waistband yet. Why, Peters, *we* don't know anything about comets, down here. If you want to see comets that *are* comets, you've got to go outside of our solar system—where there's room for them, you understand. My friend, I've seen comets out there that couldn't even lay down inside the *orbits* of our noblest comets without their tails hanging over.

Well, I boomed along another hundred and fifty million miles, and got up abreast his shoulder, as you may say. I was feeling pretty fine, I tell you; but just then I noticed the officer of the deck come to the side and hoist his glass in my direction. Straight off I heard him sing out—

"Below there, ahoy! Shake her up, shake her up! Heave on a hundred million billion tons of brimstone!"

"Ay—ay, sir!"

"Pipe the stabboard watch! All hands on deck!"

"Ay—ay, sir!"

"Send two hundred thousand million men aloft to shake out royals and sky-scrapers!"

"Ay—ay, sir!"

"Hand the stuns'ls! Hang out every rag you've got! Clothe her from stem to rudder-post!"

"Ay—ay, sir!"

In about a second I begun to see I'd woke up a pretty

ugly customer, Peters. In less than ten seconds that comet was just a blazing cloud of red-hot canvas. It was piled up into the heavens clean out of sight—the old thing seemed to swell out and occupy all space; the sulphur smoke from the furnaces—oh, well, nobody can describe the way it rolled and tumbled up into the skies, and nobody can half describe the way it smelt. Neither can anybody begin to describe the way that monstrous craft begun to crash along. And such another powpow—thousands of bo's'n's whistles screaming at once, and a crew like the populations of a hundred thousand worlds like ours all swearing at once. Well, I never heard the like of it before.

We roared and thundered along side by side, both doing our level best, because I'd never struck a comet before that could lay over me, and so I was bound to beat this one or break something. I judged I had some reputation in space, and I calculated to keep it. I noticed I wasn't gaining as fast, now, as I was before, but still I was gaining. There was a power of excitement on board the comet. Upwards of a hundred billion passengers swarmed up from below and rushed to the side and begun to bet on the race. Of course this careened her and damaged her speed. My, but wasn't the mate mad! He jumped at the crowd, with his trumpet in his hand, and sung out—

"Amidships! amidships, you———!*or I'll brain the last idiot of you!"

Well, sir, I gained and gained, little by little, till at last I went skimming sweetly by the magnificent old conflagration's nose. By this time the captain of the comet had been rousted out, and he stood there in the red glare for'ard, by the mate, in his shirt-sleeves and slippers, his hair all rats' nests and one suspender hanging, and how sick those two men did look! I just simply couldn't help putting my thumb to my nose as I glided away and singing out:

*The captain could not remember what this word was. He said it was in a foreign tongue. [M. T.]

"Ta-ta! ta-ta! Any word to send to your family?"

Peters, it was a mistake. Yes, sir, I've often regretted that —it was a mistake. You see, the captain had given up the race, but that remark was too tedious for him—he couldn't stand it. He turned to the mate, and says he—

"Have we got brimstone enough of our own to make the trip?"

"Yes, sir."

"Sure?"

"Yes, sir, more than enough."

"How much have we got in cargo for Satan?"

"Eighteen hundred thousand billion quintillions of kazarks."

"Very well, then, let his boarders freeze till the next comet comes. Lighten ship! Lively, now, lively, men! Heave the whole cargo overboard!"

Peters, look me in the eye, and be calm. I found out, over there, that a kazark is exactly the bulk of a *hundred and sixty-nine worlds like ours!* They hove all that load overboard. When it fell it wiped out a considerable raft of stars just as clean as if they'd been candles and somebody blowed them out. As for the race, that was at an end. The minute she was lightened the comet swung along by me the same as if I was anchored. The captain stood on the stern, by the after-davits, and put his thumb to his nose and sung out—

"Ta-ta! ta-ta! Maybe *you've* got some message to send your friends in the Everlasting Tropics!"

Then he hove up his other suspender and started for'ard, and inside of three-quarters of an hour his craft was only a pale torch again in the distance. Yes, it was a mistake, Peters —that remark of mine. I don't reckon I'll ever get over being sorry about it. I'd 'a' beat the bully of the firmament if I'd kept my mouth shut.

But I've wandered a little off the track of my tale; I'll get back on my course again. Now you see what kind of speed

I was making. So, as I said, when I had been tearing along this way about thirty years I begun to get uneasy. Oh, it was pleasant enough, with a good deal to find out, but then it was kind of lonesome, you know. Besides, I wanted to get somewhere. I hadn't shipped with the idea of cruising forever. First off, I liked the delay, because I judged I was going with its fire and its glare—light enough then, of course, but towards the last I begun to feel that I'd rather go to—well, most any place, so as to finish up the uncertainty.

Well, one night—it was always night, except when I was rushing by some star that was occupying the whole universe with it fire and it glare—light enough then, of course, but I necessarily left it behind in a minute or two and plunged into a solid week of darkness again. The stars ain't so close together as they look to be. Where was I? Oh yes; one night I was sailing along, when I discovered a tremendous long row of blinking lights away on the horizon ahead. As I approached, they begun to tower and swell and look like anyway. America—why, sir, America—"

"By George, I've arrived at last—and at the wrong place, just as I expected!"

Then I fainted. I don't know how long I was insensible, but it must have been a good while, for, when I came to, the darkness was all gone and there was the loveliest sunshine and the balmiest, fragrantest air in its place. And there was such a marvellous world spread out before me—such a glowing, beautiful, bewitching country. The things I took for furnaces were gates, miles high, made all of flashing jewels, and they pierced a wall of solid gold that you couldn't see the top of, nor yet the end of, in either direction. I was pointed straight for one of these gates, and a-coming like a house afire. Now I noticed that the skies were black with millions of people, pointed for those gates. What a roar they made, rushing through the air! The ground was as thick as ants with people, too—billions of them, I judge.

I lit. I drifted up to a gate with a swarm of people, and

when it was my turn the head clerk says, in a businesslike way—

"Well, quick! Where are you from?"

"San Francisco," says I.

"San Fran—*what?*" says he.

"San Francisco."

He scratched his head and looked puzzled, then he says—

"Is it a planet?"

By George, Peters, think of it! "*Planet?*" says I; "it's a city. And moreover, it's one of the biggest and finest and—"

"There, there!" says he, "no time here for conversation. We don't deal in cities here. Where are you from in a *general* way?"

"Oh," I says, "I beg your pardon. Put me down for California."

I had him *again,* Peters! He puzzled a second, then he says, sharp and irritable—

"I don't know any such planet—is it a constellation?"

"Oh, my goodness!" says I. "Constellation, says you? No—it's a State."

"Man, we don't deal in States here. *Will* you tell me where you are from *in general—at large,* don't you understand?"

"Oh, now I get your idea," I says. "I'm from America—the United States of America."

Peters, do you know I had him *again?* If I hadn't I'm a clam! His face was as blank as a target after a militia shooting-match. He turned to an under clerk and says—

"Where is America? *What* is America?"

The under clerk answered up prompt and says—

"There ain't any such orb."

"*Orb?*" says I. "Why, what are you talking about, young man? It ain't an orb; it's a country; it's a continent. Columbus discovered it; I reckon likely you've heard of *him,* anyway. America—why, sir America—"

"Silence!" says the head clerk. "Once for all, where—are—you—*from?*"

"Well," says I, "I don't know anything more to say—unless I lump things, and just say I'm from the world."

"Ah," says he, brightening up, "now that's something like! *What* world?"

Peters, he had *me*, that time. I looked at him, puzzled, he looked at me, worried. Then he burst out—

"Come, come, what world?"

Says I, "Why, *the* world, of course."

"*The* world!" he says. "H'm! there's billions of them! ... Next!"

That meant for me to stand aside. I done so, and a sky-blue man with seven heads and only one leg hopped into my place. I took a walk. It just occurred to me, then, that all the myriads I had seen swarming to that gate, up to this time, were just like that creature. I tried to run across somebody I was acquainted with, but they were out of acquaintances of mine just then. So I thought the thing all over and finally sidled back there pretty meek and feeling rather stumped, as you may say.

"Well?" said the head clerk.

"Well, sir," I says, pretty humble, "I don't seem to make out which world it is I'm from. But you may know it from this—it's the one the Saviour saved."

He bent his head at the Name. Then he says, gently—

"The worlds He has saved are like to the gates of heaven in number—none can count them. What astronomical system is your world in?—perhaps that may assist."

"It's the one that has the sun in it—and the moon—and Mars"—he shook his head at each name—hadn't ever heard of them, you see—"and Neptune—and Uranus—and Jupiter—"

"Hold on!" says he—"hold on a minute! Jupiter . . . Jupiter . . . Seems to me we had a man from there eight or nine hundred years ago—but people from that system very seldom enter by this gate." All of a sudden he begun to look me so straight in the eye that I thought he was going to bore through me. Then he says, very deliberate, "Did you come *straight here* from your system?"

"Yes, sir" I says—but I blushed the least little bit in the world when I said it.

He looked at me very stern, and says—

"That is not true; and this is not the place for prevarication. You wandered from your course. How did that happen?"

Says I, blushing again—

"I'm sorry, and I take back what I said, and confess. I raced a little with a comet one day—only just the least little bit—only the tiniest lit—"

"So—so," says he—and without any sugar in his voice to speak of.

I went on, and says—

"But I only fell off just a bare point, and I went right back on my course again the minute the race was over."

"No matter—that divergence has made all this trouble. It has brought you to a gate that is billions of leagues from the right one. If you had gone to your own gate they would have known all about your world at once and there would have been no delay. But we will try to accommodate you." He turned to an under clerk and says—

"What system is Jupiter in?"

"I don't remember, sir, but I think there is such a planet in one of the little new systems away out in one of the thinly worlded corners of the universe. I will see."

He got a balloon and sailed up and up and up, in front of a map that was as big as Rhode Island. He went on till he was out of sight, and by and by he came down and got something to eat and went up again. To cut a long story short, he kept on doing this for a day or two, and finally he came down and said he thought he had found that solar system, but it might be fly-specks. So he got a microscope and went back. It turned out better than he feared. He had rousted out our system, sure enough. He got me to describe our planet and its distance from the sun, and then he says to his chief—

"Oh, I know the one he means now, sir. It is on the map. It is called the Wart."

Says I to myself, "Young man, it wouldn't be wholesome for you to go down *there* and call it the Wart."

Well, they let me in, then, and told me I was safe forever and wouldn't have any more trouble.

Then they turned from me and went on with their work, the same as if they considered my case all complete and shipshape. I was a good deal surprised at this, but I was diffident about speaking up and reminding them. I did so hate to do it, you know; it seemed a pity to bother them, they had so much on their hands. Twice I thought I would give up and let the thing go; so twice I started to leave, but immediately I thought what a figure I should cut stepping out amongst the redeemed in such a rig, and that made me hang back and come to anchor again. People got to eying me—clerks, you know—wondering why I didn't get under way. I couldn't stand this long—it was too uncomfortable. So at last I plucked up courage and tipped the head clerk a signal. He says—

"What! you here yet? What's wanting?"

Says I, in a low voice and very confidential, making a trumpet with my hand at his ear—

"I beg pardon, and you mustn't mind my reminding you, and seeming to meddle, but hain't you forgot something?"

He studied a second, and says—

"Forgot something? ... No, not that I know of."

"Think," says I.

He thought. Then he says—

"No, I can't seem to have forgot anything. What is it?"

"Look at me," says I, "look me all over."

He done it.

"Well?" says he.

"Well," says I, "you don't notice anything? If I branched out amongst the elect looking like this, wouldn't I attract considerable attention?—wouldn't I be a little conspicuous?"

"Well," he says, "I don't see anything the matter. What do you lack?"

"Lack! Why, I lack my harp, and my wreath, and my halo, and my hymn-book, and my palm branch—I lack everything that a body naturally requires up here, my friend."

Puzzled? Peters, he was the worst puzzled man you ever saw. Finally he says—

"Well, you seem to be a curiosity every way a body takes you. I never heard of these things before."

I looked at the man awhile in solid astonishment; then I says—

"Now, I hope you don't take it as an offence, for I don't mean any, but really, for a man that has been in the Kingdom as long as I reckon you have, you do seem to know powerful little about its customs."

"Its customs!" says he. "Heaven is a large place, good friend. Large empires have many and diverse customs. Even small dominions have, as you know by what you have seen of the matter on a small scale in the Wart. How can you imagine I could ever learn the varied customs of the countless kingdoms of heaven? It makes my head ache to think of it. I know the customs that prevail in those portions inhabited by peoples that are appointed to enter by my own gate—and hark ye, that is quite enough knowledge for one individual to try to pack into his head in the thirty-seven millions of years I have devoted night and day to that study. But the idea of learning the customs of the whole appalling expanse of heaven—O man, how insanely you talk! Now I don't doubt that this odd costume you talk about is the fashion in that district of heaven you belong to, but you won't be conspicuous in this section without it."

I felt all right, if that was the case, so I bade him good-day and left. All day I walked towards the far end of a prodigious hall of the office, hoping to come out into heaven any moment, but it was a mistake. That hall was built on the general heavenly plan—it naturally couldn't be small. At last I got so tired I couldn't go any farther; so I sat down to rest, and begun to tackle the queerest sort of strangers and ask for information; but I didn't get any; they couldn't understand my language, and I could not understand theirs. I got dreadfully lonesome. I was so downhearted and homesick I wished a hundred times I never had died. I turned back, of course. About noon next day, I got back at last and was on hand at the booking-office once more. Says I to the head clerk—

"I begin to see that a man's got to be in his own heaven to be happy."

"Perfectly correct," says he. "Did you imagine the same heaven would suit all sorts of men?"

"Well, I had that idea—but I see the foolishness of it. Which way am I to go to get to my district?"

He called the under clerk that had examined the map, and he gave me general directions. I thanked him and started; but he says—

"Wait a minute; it is millions of leagues from here. Go outside and stand on that red wishing-carpet; shut your eyes, hold your breath, and wish yourself there."

"I'm much obliged," says I; "why didn't you dart me through when I first arrived?"

"We have a good deal to think of here; it was your place to think of it and ask for it. Good-by; we probably shan't see you in this region for a thousand centuries or so."

"In that case, *o revoor*," says I.

I hopped onto the carpet and held my breath and shut my eyes and wished I was in the booking-office of my own section. The very next instant a voice I knew sung out in a business kind of way—

"A harp and a hymn-book, pair of wings and a halo, size 13, for Cap'n Eli Stormfield, of San Francisco!—make him out a clean bill of health, and let him in."

I opened my eyes. Sure enough, it was a Pi Ute Injun I used to know in Tulare County; mighty good fellow—I remember being at his funeral, which consisted of him being burnt and the other Injuns gauming their faces with his ashes and howling like wildcats. He was powerful glad to see me, and you may make up your mind I was just as glad to see him, and feel that I was in the right kind of a heaven at last.

Just as far as your eye could reach, there was swarms of clerks, running and bustling around, tricking out thousands of Yanks and Mexicans and English and A-rabs, and all sorts of people in their new outfits; and when they gave me my kit and I put on my halo and took a look in the glass, I could have jumped over a house for joy, I was so happy.

"Now *this* is something like!" says I.

"Now," says I, "I'm all right—show me a cloud."

Inside of fifteen minutes I was a mile on my way towards the cloud-banks and about a million people along with me. Most of us tried to fly, but some got crippled and nobody made a success of it. So we concluded to walk, for the present, till we had had some wing practice.

We begun to meet swarms of folks who were coming back. Some had harps and nothing else; some had hymn-books and nothing else; some had nothing at all; all of them looked meek and uncomfortable; one young fellow hadn't anything left but his halo, and he was carrying that in his hand; all of a sudden he offered it to me and says—

"Will you hold it for me a minute?"

Then he disappeared in the crowd. I went on. A woman asked me to hold her palm branch, and then *she* disappeared. A girl got me to hold her harp for her, and by George, *she* disappeared; and so on and so on, till I was about loaded down to the guards. Then comes a smiling old gentleman and asked me to hold *his* things. I swabbed off the perspiration and says, pretty tart—

"I'll have to get you to excuse me, my friend,—*I* ain't no hat-rack."

About this time I begun to run across piles of those traps, lying in the road. I just quietly dumped my extra cargo along with them. I looked around, and, Peters, that whole nation that was following me were loaded down the same as I'd been. The return crowd had got them to hold their things a minute, you see. They all dumped their loads, too, and we went on.

When I found myself perched on a cloud, with a million other people, I never felt so good in my life. Says I, "Now this is according to the promises; I've been having my doubts, but now I *am* in heaven, sure enough." I gave my palm branch a wave or two, for luck, and then I tautened up my harp-strings and struck in. Well, Peters, you can't imagine anything like the row we made. It was grand to listen to, and made a body thrill all over, but there was considerable many tunes going on at once, and that was a drawback to the harmony, you understand; and then there was a lot of Injun tribes, and they kept up such another war-whooping that they kind of took the tuck out of the music. By and by I quit performing, and judged I'd take a rest. There was quite a nice mild old gentleman sitting next me, and I noticed he didn't take a hand; I encouraged him, but he said he was naturally bashful, and was afraid to try before so many people. By and by the old gentleman said he never could seem to enjoy music somehow. The fact was I was beginning to feel the same way; but I didn't say anything. Him and I had a considerable long silence, then, but of course it warn't noticeable in that place. After about sixteen or seventeen hours, during which I played and sung a little, now and then— always the same tune, because I didn't know any other— I laid down my harp and begun to fan myself with my palm branch. Then we both got to sighing pretty regular. Finally, says he—

CAPTAIN STORMFIELD'S VISIT TO HEAVEN

"Don't you know any tune but the one you've been pegging at all day?"

"Not another blessed one," says I.

"Don't you reckon you could learn another one?" says he.

"Never," says I; "I've tried to, but I couldn't manage it."

"It's a long time to hang to the one—eternity, you know."

"Don't break my heart," says I; "I'm getting low-spirited enough already."

After another long silence, says he—

"Are you glad to be here?"

Says I, "Old man, I'll be frank with you. This *ain't* just as near my idea of bliss as I thought it was going to be, when I used to go to church."

Says he, "What do you say to knocking off and calling it half a day?"

"That's me," says I. "I never wanted to get off watch so bad in my life."

So we started. Millions were coming to the cloud-bank all the time, happy and hosannahing; millions were leaving it all the time, looking mighty quiet, I tell you. We laid for the new-comers, and pretty soon I'd got them to hold my things a minute, and then I was a free man again and most outrageously happy. Just then I ran across old Sam Bartlett, who had been dead a long time, and stopped to have a talk with him.[1] Says I—

"Now tell me—is this to go on forever? Ain't there anything else for a change?"[2]

Says he—

"I'll set you right on that point very quick. People take

---

[1]MTP NB #17. May 1883-Aug. 12, 1884. Copyright The Mark Twain Company 1970. p. 21. Stormfield must hear of a man who worked hard all his life to acquire heaven; & when he got there the first person he met was a man whom he had been hoping all the time was in hell—so disappointed & outraged that he inquired the way to hell & took his satchel & left.

[2]MTP NB #17. Copyright The Mark Twain Company 1970. p. 27. Wakeman mentions a fellow who goes sneering around in heaven—nothing suits him—(hell) hl of a place, he says. Always making suggestions of improvements.

[65]

the figurative language of the Bible and the allegories for literal, and the first thing they ask for when they get here is a halo and a harp, and so on. Nothing that's harmless and reasonable is refused a body here, if he asks it in the right spirit. So they are outfitted with these things without a word. They go and sing and play just about one day, and that's the last you'll ever see them in the choir. They don't need anybody to tell them that that sort of thing wouldn't make a heaven—at least not a heaven that a sane man could stand a week and remain sane.[3] That cloud-bank is placed where the noise can't disturb the old inhabitants, and so there ain't any harm in letting everybody get up there and cure himself as soon as he comes.

"Now you just remember this—heaven is as blissful and lovely as it can be; but it's just the busiest place you ever heard of. There ain't any idle people here after the first day. Singing hymns and waving palm branches through all eternity is pretty when you hear about it in the pulpit, but it's as poor a way to put in valuable time as a body could contrive. It would just make a heaven of warbling ignoramuses, don't you see? Eternal Rest sounds comforting in the pulpit, too. Well, you try it once, and see how heavy time will hang on your hands. Why, Stormfield, a man like you, that had been active and stirring all his life, would go mad in six months in a heaven where he hadn't anything to do. Heaven is the very last place to come to *rest* in,—and don't you be afraid to bet on that!"

Says I—

"Sam, I'm as glad to hear it as I thought I'd be sorry. I'm glad I come, now."

Says he—

"Cap'n, ain't you pretty physically tired?"

Says I—

[3]MTP NB #25. Oct. 24, 1890-June 14, 1891. Copyright The Mark Twain Company 1970. p. 33. Insert chapters of Visit to Heaven—from crazy man in an Asylum at Geneva.

"Sam, it ain't any name for it! I'm dog-tired."

"Just so—just so. You've earned a good sleep, and you'll get it. You've earned a good appetite, and you'll enjoy your dinner. It's the same here as it is on earth—you've got to earn a thing, square and honest, before you enjoy it. You can't enjoy first and earn afterwards. But there's this difference, here: you can choose your own occupation, and all the powers of heaven will be put forth to help you make a success of it, if you do your level best. The shoemaker on earth that had the soul of a poet in him won't have to make shoes here."

"Now that's all reasonable and right," says I. "Plenty of work, and the kind you hanker after; no more pain, no more suffering—"

"Oh, hold on; there's plenty of pain here[4]—but it don't kill. There's plenty of suffering here, but it don't last. You see, happiness ain't a *thing in itself*—it's only a *contrast* with something that ain't pleasant. That's all it is. There ain't a thing you can mention that is happiness in its own self—it's only so by contrast with the other thing. And so, as soon as the novelty is over and the force of the contrast dulled, it ain't happiness any longer, and you have to get something fresh. Well, there's plenty of pain and suffering in heaven —consequently there's plenty of contrasts and just no end of happiness."

Says I, "It's the sensiblest heaven I've heard of yet, Sam, though it's about as different from the one I was brought up on as a live princess is different from her own wax figger."

Along in the first months I knocked around about the Kingdom, making friends and finally settled down in a pretty

[4]MTP NB #17. Copyright The Mark Twain Company 1970. p. 22. Capt. S finds that Hell was originally instituted in deference to an early Christian sentiment. In modern times the halls of heaven are warmed by registers connected with hell—& it is greatly applauded by Jonathan Edwards, Calvin, Baxter & Co because it adds a new pang to the sinner's sufferings to know that the (f) very fire which tortures him is the means of making the righteous comfortable.

likely region, to have a rest before taking another start. I went on making acquaintances and gathering up information. I had a good deal of talk with an old bald-headed angel by the name of Sandy McWilliams. He was from somewhere in New Jersey. I went about with him, considerable. We used to lay around, warm afternoons, in the shade of a rock, on some meadow-ground that was pretty high and out of the marshy slush of his cranberry-farm, and there we used to talk about all kinds of things and smoke pipes. One day, says I—

"About how old might you be, Sandy?"

"Seventy-two."

"I judged so. How long you been in heaven?"

"Twenty-seven years, come Christmas."

"How old was you when you come up?"

"Why, seventy-two, of course."

"You can't mean it!"

"Why can't I mean it!"

"Because, if you was seventy-two then, you are naturally ninety-nine now."

"No, but I ain't. I stay the same age I was when I come."

"Well," says I, "come to think, there's something just here that I want to ask about. Down below, I always had an idea that in heaven we would all be young, and bright, and spry."

"Well, you *can* be young if you want to. You've only got to wish."

"Well, then why didn't you wish?"

"I did. They all did. You'll try it, some day, like enough; but you'll get tired of the change pretty soon."

"Why?"

"Well, I'll tell you. Now you've always been a sailor; did you ever try some other business?"

"Yes, I tried keeping grocery, once, up in the mines; but I couldn't stand it; it was too dull—no stir, no storm, no life about it; it was like being part dead and part alive, both at the same time. I wanted to be one thing or t'other. I shut up shop pretty quick and went to sea."

"That's it. Grocery people like it, but you couldn't. You see you wasn't used to it. Well, I wasn't used to being young, and I couldn't seem to take any interest in it. I was strong, and handsome, and had curly hair,—yes, and wings, too!—gay wings like a butterfly. I went to picnics and dances and parties with the fellows, and tried to carry on and talk nonsense with the girls, but it wasn't any use; I couldn't take to it—fact is, it was an awful bore. What I wanted was early to bed and early to rise, and something to *do;* and when my work was done, I wanted to sit quiet, and smoke and think—not tear around with a parcel of giddy young kids. You can't think what I suffered whilst I was young."

"How long was you young?"

"Only two weeks. That was plenty for me. Laws, I was so lonesome! You see, I was full of the knowledge and experience of seventy-two years; the deepest subject those young folks could strike was only *a-b-c* to me. And to hear them argue—oh, my! it would have been funny, if it hadn't been so pitiful. Well, I was so hungry for the ways and the sober talk I was used to, that I tried to ring in with the old people, but they wouldn't have it. They considered me a conceited young upstart, and gave me the cold shoulder. Two weeks was a-plenty for me. I was glad to get back my bald head again, and my pipe, and my old drowsy reflections in the shade of a rock or a tree."

"Well," says I, "do you mean to say you're going to stand still at seventy-two, forever?"

"I don't know, and I ain't particular. But I ain't going to drop back to twenty-five any more—I know that, mighty well. I know a sight more than I did twenty-seven years ago, and I enjoy learning, all the time, but I don't seem to get any older. That is, bodily—my mind gets older, and stronger, and better seasoned, and more satisfactory."

Says I, "If a man comes here at ninety, don't he ever set himself back?"

"Of course he does. He sets himself back to fourteen; tries it a couple of hours, and feels like a fool; sets himself forward to twenty; it ain't much improvement; tries thirty, fifty, eighty, and finally ninety—finds he is more at home and comfortable at the same old figure he is used to than any other way. Or, if his mind begun to fail him on earth at eighty, that's where he finally sticks up here. He sticks at the place where his mind was last at its best, for there's where his enjoyment is best, and his ways most set and established."

"Does a chap of twenty-five stay always twenty-five, and look it?"

"If he is a fool, yes. But if he is bright, and ambitious and industrious, the knowledge he gains and the experiences he has, change his ways and thoughts and likings, and make him find his best pleasure in the company of people above that age; so he allows his body to take on that look of as many added years as he needs to make him comfortable and proper in that sort of society; he lets his body go on taking the look of age, according as he progresses, and by and by he will be bald and wrinkled outside, and wise and deep within."

"Babies the same?"

"Babies the same. Laws, what asses we used to be, on earth, about these things! We said we'd be always young in heaven. We didn't say *how* young—we didn't think of that, perhaps—that is, we didn't all think alike, anyway. When I was a boy of seven, I suppose I thought we'd all be twelve, in heaven; when I was twelve, I suppose I thought we'd all be eighteen or twenty in heaven; when I was forty, I begun to go back; I remember I hoped we'd all be about *thirty* years old in heaven. Neither a man nor a boy ever thinks the age he *has* is exactly the best one—he puts the *right* age a few years older or a few years younger than he is. Then he makes that ideal age the general age of the heavenly people. And he expects everybody to *stick* at that age—stand stock-still—and expects them to enjoy it!—Now just think of the idea of standing still in heaven! Think of a heaven made up entirely of hoop-rolling, marble-playing cubs of seven years!—or of awkward, diffident, sentimental immaturities of nineteen—or of vigorous people of thirty, healthy-minded, brimming with ambition, but chained hand and foot to that one age and its limitations like so many galley-slaves! Think of the dull sameness of a society made up of people all of one age and one set of looks, habits, tastes and feelings. Think how superior to it earth would be, with its variety of types and faces and ages, and the enlivening attrition of the myriad interests that come into pleasant collision in such a variegated society."

"Look here," says I, "do you know what you're doing?"

"Well, what am I doing?"

"You are making heaven pretty comfortable in one way, but you are playing the mischief with it in another."[5]

"How d'you mean?"

"Well," I says, "take a young mother that's lost her child, and—"

" 'Sh!" he says. "Look!"

It was a woman. Middle-aged, and had grizzled hair. She was walking slow, and her head was bent down, and her wings hanging limp and droopy; and she looked ever so tired, and was crying, poor thing! She passed along by, with her head down, that way, and the tears running down her face, and didn't see us. Then Sandy said, low and gentle, and full of pity:

"*She's* hunting for her child! No, *found* it, I reckon. Lord, how she's changed! But I recognized her in a minute, though it's twenty-seven years since I saw her. A young mother she was, about twenty-two or four, or along there; and blooming

[5]For a parallel reading see Appendix B.

and lovely and sweet! oh, just a flower! And all her heart and all her soul was wrapped up in her child, her little girl, two years old. And it died, and she went wild with grief, just wild! Well, the only comfort she had was that she'd see her child again, in heaven—'never more to part,' she said, and kept on saying it over and over, 'never more to part.' And the words made her happy; yes, they did; they made her joyful; and when I was dying, twenty-seven years ago, she told me to find her child the first thing, and say she was coming—'soon, soon, *very* soon, she hoped and believed!' "[6]

"Why, it's pitiful, Sandy."

He didn't say anything for a while, but sat looking at the ground, thinking. Then he says, kind of mournful:

"And now she's come!"

"Well? Go on."

"Stormfield, maybe she hasn't found the child, but *I* think she has. Looks so to me. I've seen cases before. You see, she's kept that child in her head just the same as it was when she jounced it in her arms a little chubby thing. But here it didn't elect to *stay* a child. No, it elected to grow up, which it did. And in these twenty-seven years it has learned all the deep scientific learning there *is* to learn, and is studying and studying and learning and learning more and more, all the time, and don't give a damn for anything *but* learning; just learning, and discussing gigantic problems with people like herself."

"Well?"

[6]MTP NB #32a (I). Jan. 7, 1897-June 15, 1897. Copyright The Mark Twain Company 1970. p. 3. Write a novel in which part of the action takes place in heaven & hell, the rest upon earth. Let a woman in heaven watch the sweep of the ocean of fire at close quarters—a person passes by at very long intervals only, the ocean is so large. It is a solitude—so is heaven. She has sought her daughter for a long time—she is watching hell, now, but not expecting her daughter to be there. Musing she hears a shriek & her daughter sweeps by—there is an instant of recognition by both—the mother springs in, perceiving that there is no happiness in heaven for her any longer.

"Stormfield, don't you see? Her mother knows *cranberries*, and how to tend them, and pick them, and put them up, and market them; and not another blamed thing! Her and her daughter can't be any more company for each other *now* than mud turtle and bird o' paradise. Poor thing, she was looking for a baby to jounce; *I* think she's struck a disapp'intment."

"Sandy, what will they do—stay unhappy forever in heaven?"

"No, they'll come together and get adjusted by and by. But not this year, and not next. By and by."

CHAPTER IV

I HAD BEEN HAVING considerable trouble with my wings. The day after I helped the choir I made a dash or two with them, but was not lucky. First off, I flew thirty yards, and then fouled an Irishman and brought him down —brought us both down, in fact.[7] Next, I had a collision with a Bishop—and bowled him down, of course. We had some sharp words, and I felt pretty cheap, to come banging into a grave old person like that, with a million strangers looking on and smiling to themselves.

I saw I hadn't got the hang of the steering, and so couldn't rightly tell where I was going to bring up when I started. I went afoot the rest of the day, and let my wings hang. Early next morning I went to a private place to have some practice. I got up on a pretty high rock, and got a good start, and went swooping down, aiming for a bush a little over three hundred yards off; but I couldn't seem to calculate for the wind, which was about two points abaft my beam. I could see I was going considerable to looard of the bush, so I worked my starboard wing slow and went ahead strong on the port one, but it wouldn't answer; I could see I was going to broach to, so I slowed down on both, and lit. I went back to the rock and took another chance at it. I aimed two or three points to starboard of the bush—yes, more than that—enough so as to make it nearly a head-wind. I done well enough, but made pretty poor time. I could see, plain enough, that on a head-wind, wings was a mistake. I could see that a body could sail pretty close to the wind, but he couldn't go in the wind's eye. I could see that if I wanted

---

[7] MTP NB #12. Nov. 23, 1877-78. Copyright The Mark Twain Company 1970. p. 4. March 20. An awkward new arrival brushes Wakeman in the eye with his wing.

to go a-visiting any distance from home, and the wind was ahead, I might have to wait days, maybe, for a change; and I could see, too, that these things could not be any use at all in a gale; if you tried to run before the wind, you would make a mess of it, for there isn't any way to shorten sail—like reefing, you know—you have to take it *all* in—shut your feathers down flat to your sides. That would *land* you, of course. You could lay to, with your head to the wind—that is the best you could do, and right hard work you'd find it, too. If you tried any other game, you would founder, sure.

I judge it was about a couple of weeks or so after this that I dropped old Sandy McWilliams a note one day—it was a Tuesday—and asked him to come over and take his manna and quails with me next day; and the first thing he did when he stepped in was to twinkle his eye in a sly way, and say—

"Well, Cap, what you done with your wings?"

I saw in a minute that there was some sarcasm done up in that rag somewheres, but I never let on. I only says—

"Gone to the wash."

"Yes," he says, in a dry sort of way, "they mostly go to the wash—about this time—I've often noticed it. Fresh angels are powerful neat. When do you look for 'em back?"

"Day after to-morrow," says I.

He winked at me, and smiled.

Says I—

"Sandy, out with it. Come—no secrets among friends. I notice you don't ever wear wings—and plenty others don't. I've been making an ass of myself—is that it?"

"That is about the size of it. But it is no harm. We all do it at first. It's perfectly natural. You see, on earth we jump to such foolish conclusions as to things up here. In the pictures we always saw the angels with wings on—and that was all right; but we jumped to the conclusion that that was their way of getting around—and that was all wrong. The wings ain't anything but a uniform, that's all. When they are in the field—so to speak,—they always wear them; you never see an angel going with a message anywhere without his wings, any more than you would see a military officer presiding at a court-martial without his uniform, or a postman delivering letters, or a policeman walking his beat, in plain clothes. But they ain't to *fly* with! The wings are for show, not for use. Old experienced angels are like officers of the regular army—they dress plain, when they are off duty. New angels are like the militia—never shed the uniform—always fluttering and floundering around in their wings, butting people down, flapping here, and there, and everywhere, always imagining they are attracting the admiring eye—well, they just think they are the very most important people in heaven. And when you see one of them come sailing around with one wing tipped up and t'other down, you make up your mind he is saying to himself: 'I wish Mary Ann in Arkansaw could see me now. I reckon she'd wish she hadn't shook me.' No, they're just for show, that's all—only just for show."

"I judge you've got it about right, Sandy," says I.

"Why, look at it yourself," says he. "*You* ain't built for wings—no man is. You know what a grist of years it took you to come here from the earth—and yet you were booming along faster than any cannon-ball could go. Suppose you had to fly that distance with your wings—wouldn't eternity have been over before you got here? Certainly. Well, angels have to go to the earth every day—millions of them—to appear in visions to dying children and good people, you know—it's the heft of their business. They appear with their wings, of course, because they are on official service, and because the dying persons wouldn't know they were angels if they hadn't wings—but do you reckon they fly with them? It stands to reason they don't. The wings would wear out before they got half-way; even the pin-feathers would be gone; the wing frames would be as bare as kite sticks before the paper is pasted on. The distances in heaven are billions of times greater, angels have to go all over heaven every day; could they do it with their wings alone? No, indeed; they wear the wings for style, but they travel any distance in an instant by *wishing*. The wishing-carpet of the Arabian Nights was a sensible idea—but our earthly idea of angels flying these awful distances with their clumsy wings was foolish.

"Our young saints, of both sexes, wear wings all the time—blazing red ones, and blue and green, and gold, and variegated, and rainbowed, and ring-streaked-and-striped ones—and nobody finds fault. It is suitable to their time of life. The things are beautiful, and they set the young people off. They are the most striking and lovely part of their outfit—a halo don't *begin*."

"Well," says I, "I've tucked mine away in the cupboard, and I allow to let them lay there till there's mud."

"Yes—or a reception."

"What's that?"

"Well, you can see one to-night if you want to. There's a barkeeper from Jersey City going to be received."

"Go on—tell me about it."

"This barkeeper got converted at a Moody and Sankey meeting, in New York, and started home on the ferry-boat, and there was a collision and he got drowned. He is of a class that think all heaven goes wild with joy when a particularly hard lot like him is saved; they think all heaven turns out hosannahing to welcome them; they think there isn't anything talked about in the realms of the blest but their case, for that day. This barkeeper thinks there hasn't been such another stir here in years, as his coming is going to raise.—And I've always noticed this peculiarity about a dead barkeeper—he not only expects all hands to turn out when he arrives, but he expects to be received with a torch-light procession."

"I reckon he is disappointed, then."

"No, he isn't. No man is allowed to be disappointed here.

Whatever he wants, when he comes—that is, any reasonable and unsacrilegious thing—he can have. There's always a few millions or billions of young folks around who don't want any better entertainment than to fill up their lungs and swarm out with their torches and have a high time over a barkeeper. It tickles the barkeeper till he can't rest, it makes a charming lark for the young folks, it don't do anybody any harm, it don't cost a rap, and it keeps up the place's reputation for making all comers happy and content."

"Very good. I'll be on hand and see them land the barkeeper."

"It is manners to go in full dress. You want to wear your wings, you know, and your other things."

"Which ones?"

"Halo, and harp, and palm branch, and all that."

"Well," says I, "I reckon I ought to be ashamed of myself, but the fact is I left them laying around that day I resigned from the choir. I haven't got a rag to wear but this robe and the wings."

"That's all right. You'll find they've been raked up and saved for you. Send for them."

"I'll do it, Sandy. But what was it you was saying about unsacrilegious things, which people expect to get, and will be disappointed about?"

"Oh, there are a lot of such things that people expect and don't get. For instance, there's a Brooklyn preacher by the name of Talmage, who is laying up a considerable disappointment for himself. He says, every now and then in his sermons, that the first thing he does when he gets to heaven, will be to fling his arms around Abraham, Isaac and Jacob, and kiss them and weep on them. There's millions of people down there on earth that are promising themselves the same thing. As many as sixty thousand people arrive here every single day, that want to run straight to Abraham, Isaac and Jacob, and hug them and weep on them. Now mind you, sixty thousand a day is a pretty heavy contract for those old people. If they were a mind to allow it, they wouldn't ever have anything to do, year in and year out, but stand up and be hugged and wept on thirty-two hours in the twenty-four. They would be tired out and as wet as muskrats all the time. What would heaven be, to *them?* It would be a mighty good place to get out of—you know that, yourself. Those are kind and gentle old Jews, but they ain't any fonder of kissing the emotional highlights of Brooklyn than you be. You mark my words, Mr. T.'s endearments are going to be declined, with thanks. There are limits to the privileges of the elect, even in heaven. Why, if Adam was to show himself to every new comer that wants to call and gaze at him and strike him for his autograph, he would never have time to do anything else but just that. Talmage has said he is going to give Adam some of his attentions, as well as A., I. and J. But he will have to change his mind about that."

"Do you think Talmage will really come here?"

"Why, certainly, he will; but don't you be alarmed; he will run with his own kind, and there's plenty of them. That is the main charm of heaven—there's all kinds here—which wouldn't be the case if you let the preachers tell it. Anybody can find the sort he prefers, here, and he just lets the others alone, and they let him alone. When the Deity builds a heaven, it is built right, and on a liberal plan."

Sandy sent home for his things, and I sent for mine, and about nine in the evening we begun to dress. Sandy says—

"This is going to be a grand time for you, Stormy. Like as not some of the patriarchs will turn out."

"No, but will they?"

"Like as not. Of course they are pretty exclusive. They hardly ever show themselves to the common public. I believe they never turn out except for an eleventh-hour convert. They wouldn't do it then, only earthly tradition makes a grand show pretty necessary on that kind of an occasion."

"Do they all turn out, Sandy?"

"Who?—all the patriarchs? Oh, no—hardly ever more than a couple. You will be here fifty thousand years—maybe more—before you get a glimpse of all the patriarchs and prophets. Since I have been here, Job has been to the front once, and once Ham and Jeremiah both at the same time. But the finest thing that has happened in my day was a year or so ago; that was Charles Peace's reception—him they called 'the Bannercross Murderer'—an Englishman. There were four patriarchs and two prophets on the Grand Stand that time—there hasn't been anything like it since Captain Kidd came; Abel was there—the first time in twelve hundred years. A report got around that Adam was coming; well, of course, Abel was enough to bring a crowd, all by himself, but there is nobody that can draw like Adam. It was a false report, but it got around, anyway, as I say, and it will be a long day before I see the like of it again. The reception was in the English department, of course, which is eight hundred and eleven million miles from the New Jersey line. I went, along with a good many of my neighbors, and it was a sight to see, I can tell you. Flocks came from all the departments. I saw Esquimaux there, and Tartars, negroes, Chinamen—people from everywhere.[8] You see a mixture like that in the Grand Choir, the first day you land here, but you hardly ever see it again. There were billions of people; when they were singing or hosannahing,

---

[8]MTP NB #15. July 26, 1880-Dec. 1881. Copyright The Mark Twain Company 1970. pp. 7-8. Early, in heaven Stormfield is delighted with the social equalities—a nigger, a (Chinaman,) Digger, an esquimaux, and a (Nasty Frenchman) Fejeean—invite themselves to dinner with him—"if we had another animal or two, we could start a menagerie." Next time, they bring also an orang-outang. "The (mag) menag. progresses." Next time they bring also a Frenchman. "The menagerie is complete," says Stormy. But next time they brought also a French married lady. "This is carrying it too far; this will not answer; I have read enough French novels to know that a French married lady cannot enter even a menagerie without bringing the purity of that menagerie under suspicion." It was proposed to (bring) substitute a French maiden of 12, or one of 75. "No, it would not be the best for the menagerie. The French confess, by the strict guard they keep (of) over their maidens of all ages, (and all

the noise was wonderful; and even when their tongues were still the drumming of the wings was nearly enough to burst your head, for all the sky was as thick as if it was snowing angels. Although Adam was not there, it was a great time anyway, because we had three archangels on the Grand Stand—it is a seldom thing that even one comes out."

"What did they look like, Sandy?"

"Well, they had shining faces, and shining robes, and wonderful rainbow wings, and they stood eighteen feet high, and wore swords, and held their heads up in a noble way, and looked like soldiers."

"Did they have halos?"

"No—anyway, not the hoop kind. The archangels and the upper-class patriarchs wear a finer thing than that. It is a round, solid, splendid glory of gold, that is blinding to look at. You have often seen a patriarch in a picture, on earth, with that thing on—you remember it?—he looks as if he had his head in a brass platter. That don't give you the right idea of it at all—it is much more shining and beautiful."

"Did you talk with those archangels and patriarchs, Sandy?"

"Who—*I*? Why, what can you be thinking about, Stormy? I ain't worthy to speak to such as they."

"Is Talmage?"

"Of course not. You have got the same mixed-up idea about these things that everybody has down there. I had it

---

stages of) that they cannot be trusted. Their novels are everywhere—nothing could prevent their girls from reading them; they do read them; consequently whilst they are chaste in body, through compulsion, they are unchaste in mind. Let us keep the menagerie pure, from the American point of view, not the French. (No, we will have no) That is to say, let us have real, not sham, purity."

The menag. continued to grow, till it had in it cannibals, Presbyterians, pariahs, politicians, (teetotalers,) Turks, tramps—indeed, all sorts of disagreeable people; and they all called him "Brother Stormfield" and kept falling on his neck and weeping down his back in pious joy. Finally he said "Heaven is a most unpleasant place; there is no privacy in it. I must move."

once, but I got over it. Down there they talk of the heavenly King—and that is right—but then they go right on speaking as if this was a republic[9] and everybody was on a dead level with everybody else, and privileged to fling his arms around anybody he comes across, and be hail-fellow-well-met[10] with all the elect, from the highest down. How tangled up and absurd that is! How are you going to have a republic under a king? How are you going to have a republic at all, where the head of the government is absolute, holds his place forever, and has no parliament, no council to meddle or make in his affairs, nobody voted for, nobody elected, nobody in the whole universe with a voice in the government, nobody asked to take a hand in its matters, and nobody *allowed* to do it? Fine republic, ain't it?"

"Well, yes—it *is* a little different from the idea I had—but I thought I might go around and get acquainted with the grandees, anyway—not exactly splice the main-brace with them, you know, but shake hands and pass the time of day."

"Could Tom, Dick and Harry call on the Cabinet of Russia and do that?—on Prince Gortschakoff, for instance?"

"I reckon not, Sandy."

"Well, this is Russia—only more so. There's not the shadow of a republic about it anywhere. There are ranks, here. There are viceroys, princes, governors, sub-governors, sub-sub-governors, and a hundred orders of nobility, grad-

---

[9] MTP NB #12. Nov. 23, 1877-78. Copyright The Mark Twain Company 1970. p. 16, 22d Apl. Have some people (an) dissatisfied because Heaven is an absolute monarchy, with many viceroys, when they expected a leatherheaded Republic with the damnation of unrestricted suffrage. [(Capt. Stormfield, SLC to WDH 6/27/78)]

[10] [Talking about things in general, or at least another subject] Do you forget that heaven is packed with a multitude of all nations and that these people are all on the most familiar how-the-hell-are-you footing with Talmadge swinging around the circle to all eternity hugging the saints and patriarchs and archangels, and forcing you to do the same unless you choose to make yourself an object of remark if you refrain? Then why do you try to get to heaven? Be warned in time.

SLC to WDH. March 1, 1883. Correspondence I, 427.

ing along down from grand-ducal archangels, stage by stage, till the general level is struck, where there ain't any titles. Do you know what a prince of the blood is, on earth?"

"No."

"Well, a prince of the blood don't belong to the royal family exactly, and he don't belong to the mere nobility of the kingdom; he is lower than the one, and higher than t'other. That's about the position of the patriarchs and prophets here. There's some mighty high nobility here—people that you and I ain't worthy to polish sandals for—and *they* ain't worthy to polish sandals for the patriarchs and prophets. That gives you a kind of an idea of their rank, don't it? You begin to see how high up they are, don't you? Just to get a two-minute glimpse of one of them is a thing for a body to remember and tell about for a thousand years. Why, Captain, just think of this: if Abraham was to set foot down here by this door, there would be a railing set up around that foot-track right away, and a shelter put over it, and people would flock here from all over heaven, for hundreds and hundreds of years, to look at it. Abraham is one of the parties that Mr. Talmage, of Brooklyn, is going to embrace, and kiss, and weep on, when he comes. He wants to lay in a good stock of tears, you know, or five to one he will go dry before he gets a chance to do it."

"Sandy," says I, "I had an idea that *I* was going to be equals with everybody here, too, but I will let that drop. It don't matter, and I am plenty happy enough anyway."

"Captain, you are happier than you would be, the other way. These old patriarchs and prophets have got ages the start of you; they know more in two minutes than you know in a year. Did you ever try to have a sociable improving-time discussing winds, and currents and variations of compass with an undertaker?"

"I get your idea, Sandy. He couldn't interest me. He would be an ignoramus in such things—he would bore me, and I would bore him."

"You have got it. You would bore the patriarchs when you talked, and when they talked they would shoot over your head. By and by you would say, 'Good morning, your Eminence,[11] I will call again'—but you wouldn't. Did you ever ask the slush-boy to come up in the cabin and take dinner with you?"

"I get your drift again, Sandy. I wouldn't be used to such grand people as the patriarchs and prophets, and I would be sheepish and tongue-tied in their company, and mighty glad to get out of it. Sandy, which is the highest rank, patriarch or prophet?"

"Oh, the prophets hold over the patriarchs. The newest prophet, even, is of a sight more consequence than the oldest patriarch. Yes, sir, Adam himself has to walk behind Shakespeare."

"Was Shakespeare a prophet?"

"Of course he was; and so was Homer, and heaps more. But Shakespeare and the rest have to walk behind a common tailor from Tennessee, by the name of Billings; and behind a horse-doctor named Sakka, from Afghanistan. Jeremiah, and Billings and Buddha walk together, side by side, right behind a crowd from planets not in our astronomy; next come a dozen or two from Jupiter and other worlds; next come Daniel, and Sakka and Confucius; next a lot from systems outside of ours; next come Ezekiel, and Mahomet, Zoroaster, and a knife-grinder from ancient Egypt; then there is a long string, and after them, away down toward the bottom, come Shakespeare and Homer, and a shoemaker named Marais, from the back settlements of France."

"Have they really rung in Mahomet and all those other heathens?"

"Yes—they all had their message, and they all get their

---

[11]MTP NB #22. Nov. 1887-June, 1888. Copyright The Mark Twain Company 1970. p. 64. No, there is no reverence with us. I remember once in a dream I went to heaven, & noticed there that it was an ordinary thing for Americans to hail Michael the archangel as he went by with a hearty & friendly "Hello, Mike!"

[84]

reward. The man who don't get his reward on earth, needn't bother—he will get it here, sure."

"But why did they throw off on Shakespeare, that way, and put him away down there below those shoemakers and horse-doctors and knife-grinders—a lot of people nobody ever heard of?"

"That is the heavenly justice of it—they warn't rewarded according to their deserts, on earth, but here they get their rightful rank. That tailor Billings, from Tennessee, wrote poetry that Homer and Shakespeare couldn't begin to come up to; but nobody would print it, nobody read it but his neighbors, an ignorant lot, and they laughed at it. Whenever the village had a drunken frolic and a dance, they would drag him in and crown him with cabbage leaves, and pretend to bow down to him; and one night when he was sick and nearly starved to death, they had him out and crowned him, and then they rode him on a rail about the village, and everybody followed along, beating tin pans and yelling. Well, he died before morning. He wasn't ever expecting to go to heaven, much less that there was going to be any fuss made over him, so I reckon he was a good deal surprised when the reception broke on him."

"Was you there, Sandy?"

"Bless you, no!"

"Why? Didn't you know it was going to come off?"

"Well, I judge I did. It was the talk of these realms—not for a day, like this barkeeper business, but for twenty years before the man died."

"Why the mischief didn't you go, then?"

"Now how you talk! The like of me go meddling around at the reception of a prophet? A mudsill like me trying to push in and help receive an awful grandee like Edward J. Billings? Why, I should have been laughed at for a billion miles around. I shouldn't ever heard the last of it."

"Well, who did go, then?"

"Mighty few people that you and I will ever get a chance

to see, Captain. Not a solitary commoner ever has the luck to see a reception of a prophet, I can tell you. All the nobility, and all the patriarchs and prophets—every last one of them—and all the archangels, and all the princes and governors and viceroys, were there,—and *no* small fry—not a single one. And mind you, I'm not talking about only the grandees from *our* world, but the princes and patriarchs and so on from *all* the worlds that shine in our sky, and from billions more that belong in systems upon systems away outside of the one our sun is in. There were some prophets and patriarchs there that ours ain't a circumstance to, for rank and illustriousness and all that. Some were from Jupiter and other worlds in our own system, but the most celebrated were three poets, Saa, Bo and Soof, from great planets in three different and very remote systems. These three names are common and familiar in every nook and corner of heaven, clear from one end of it to the other—fully as well known as the eighty Supreme Archangels, in fact—whereas our Moses, and Adam, and the rest, have not been heard of outside of our world's little corner of heaven, except by a few very learned men scattered here and there—and they always spell their names wrong, and get the performances of one mixed up with the doings of another, and they almost always locate them simply *in our solar system*, and think that is enough without going into little details such as naming the particular world they are from. It is like a learned Hindoo showing off how much he knows by saying Longfellow lives in the United States—as if he lived all over the United States, and as if the country was so small you couldn't throw a brick there without hitting him. Between you and me, it does gravel me, the cool way people from those monster worlds outside our system snub our little world, and even our system. Of course we think a good deal of Jupiter, because our world is only a potato to it, for size; but then there are worlds in other systems that Jupiter isn't even a mustard-seed to—like the planet Goobra, for instance, which you couldn't squeeze inside the orbit of Halley's comet without straining the rivets. Tourists from Goobra (I mean parties that lived and died there—natives) come here, now and then, and inquire about our world, and when they find out it is so little that a streak of lightning can flash clear around it in the eighth of a second, they have to lean up against something to laugh. Then they screw a glass into their eye and go to examining *us*, as if we were a curious kind of foreign bug, or something of that sort. One of them asked me how long our day was; and when I told him it was twelve hours long, as a general thing, he asked me if people where I was from considered it worth while to get up and wash for such a day as that. That is the way with those Goobra people—they can't seem to let a chance go by to throw it in your face that their day is three hundred and twenty-two of our years long. This young snob was just of age—he was six or seven thousand of his days old—say two million of our years— and he had all the puppy airs that belong to that time of life—that turning-point when a person has got over being a boy and yet ain't quite a man exactly. If it had been anywhere else but in heaven, I would have given him a piece of my mind. Well, anyway, Billings had the grandest reception that has been seen in thousands of centuries, and I think it will have a good effect. His name will be carried pretty far, and it will make our system talked about, and maybe our world, too, and raise us in the respect of the general public of heaven. Why, look here—Shakespeare walked backwards before that tailor from Tennessee, and scattered flowers for him to walk on, and Homer stood behind his chair and waited on him at the banquet. Of course that didn't go for much *there*, amongst all those big foreigners from other systems, as they hadn't heard of Shakespeare or Homer either, but it would amount to considerable down there on our little earth if they could know about it. I wish there was something *in* that miserable spiritualism, so we could send them word. That Tennessee village would set up a monument to

Billings, then, and his autograph would outsell Satan's. Well, they had grand times at that reception—a small-fry noble from Hoboken told me all about it—Sir Richard Duffer, Baronet."

"What, Sandy, a nobleman from Hoboken? How is that?"

"Easy enough. Duffer kept a sausage-shop and never saved a cent in his life because he used to give all his spare meat to the poor, in a quiet way. Not tramps—no, the other sort—the sort that will starve before they will beg—honest square people out of work. Dick used to watch hungry-looking men and women and children, and track them home, and find out all about them from the neighbors, and then feed them and find them work. As nobody ever *saw* him give anything to anybody, he had the reputation of being mean; he died with it, too, and everybody said it was a good riddance; but the minute he landed here, they made him a baronet, and the very first words Dick the sausage-maker of Hoboken heard when he stepped upon the heavenly shore were, 'Welcome, Sir Richard Duffer!' It surprised him some, because he thought he had reasons to believe he was pointed for a warmer climate than this one."

All of a sudden the whole region fairly rocked under the crash of eleven hundred and one thunder blasts, all let off at once, and Sandy says—

"There, that's for the barkeep."

I jumped up and says—

"Then let's be moving along, Sandy; we don't want to miss any of this thing, you know."

"Keep your seat," he says; "he is only just telegraphed, that is all."

"How?"

"That blast only means that he has been sighted from the signal-station. He is off Sandy Hook. The committees will go down to meet him, now, and escort him in. There will be ceremonies and delays; they won't be coming up the

Bay for a considerable time, yet. It is several billion miles away, anyway."

"*I* could have been a barkeeper and a hard lot just as well as not," says I, remembering the lonesome way I arrived, and how there wasn't any committee nor anything.

"I notice some regret in your voice," says Sandy, "and it is natural enough; but let bygones be bygones; you went according to your lights, and it is too late now to mend the thing."

"No, let it slide, Sandy, I don't mind. But you've got a Sandy Hook *here*, too, have you?"

"We've got everything here, just as it is below. All the States and Territories of the Union, and all the kingdoms of the earth and the islands of the sea are laid out here just as they are on the globe—all the same shape they are down there, and all graded to the relative size, only each State and realm and island is a good many billion times bigger here than it is below. There goes another blast."

"What is that one for?"

"That is only another fort answering the first one. They each fire eleven hundred and one thunder blasts at a single dash—it is the usual salute for an eleventh-hour guest; a hundred for each hour and an extra one for the guest's sex; if it was a woman we would know it by their leaving off the extra gun."

"How do we know there's eleven hundred and one, Sandy, when they all go off at once?—and yet we certainly do know."

"Our intellects are a good deal sharpened up, here, in some ways, and that is one of them. Numbers and sizes and distances are so great, here, that we have to be made so we can *feel* them—our old ways of counting and measuring and ciphering wouldn't ever give us an idea of them, but would only confuse us and oppress us and make our heads ache."

After some more talk about this, I says: "Sandy, I notice that I hardly ever see a white angel; where I run across one white angel, I strike as many as a hundred million copper-colored ones—people that can't speak English. How is that?"

"Well, you will find it the same in any State or Territory of the American corner of heaven you choose to go to. I have shot along, a whole week on a stretch, and gone millions and millions of miles, through perfect swarms of angels, without ever seeing a single white one, or hearing a word I could understand. You see, America was occupied a billion years and more, by Injuns and Aztecs, and that sort of folks, before a white man ever set his foot in it. During the first three hundred years after Columbus's discovery, there wasn't ever more than one good lecture audience of white people, all put together, in America—I mean the whole thing, British Possessions and all; in the beginning of our century there were only 6,000,000 or 7,000,000—say seven; 12,000,000 or 14,000,000 in 1825; say 23,000,000 in 1850; 40,000,000 in 1875. Our death-rate has always been 20 in 1000 per annum. Well, 140,000 died the first year of the century; 280,000 the twenty-fifth year; 500,000 the fiftieth year; about a million the seventy-fifth year. Now I am going to be liberal about this thing, and consider that fifty million whites have died in America from the beginning up to today—make it sixty, if you want to; make it a hundred million—it's no difference about a few millions one way or t'other. Well, now, you can see, yourself, that when you come to spread a little dab of people like that over these hundreds of billions of miles of American territory here in heaven, it is like scattering a ten-cent box of homeopathic pills over the Great Sahara and expecting to find them again. You can't expect us to amount to anything in heaven, and we *don't*—now that is the simple fact, and we have got to do the best we can with it. The learned men from other planets and other systems come here and hang around a while, when they are touring around the Kingdom, and then go back to their own section of heaven and write a book of travels, and they give America about five lines in it. And what do they say about us? They say this wilderness is populated with a scattering few hundred thousand billions of red angels, with now and then a curiously complected *diseased* one. You see, they think we whites and the occasional nigger are Injuns that have been bleached out or blackened by some leprous disease or other—for some peculiarly rascally *sin,* mind you. It is a mighty sour pill for us all, my friend—even the modestest of us, let alone the other kind, that think they are going to be received like a long-lost government bond, and hug Abraham into the bargain. I haven't asked you any of the particulars, Captain, but I judge it goes without saying—if my experience is worth anything—that there wasn't much of a hooraw made over you when you arrived—now was there?"

"Don't mention it, Sandy," says I, coloring up a little; "I wouldn't have had the family see it for any amount you are a mind to name. Change the subject, Sandy, change the subject."

"Well, do you think of settling in the California department of bliss?"

"I don't know. I wasn't calculating on doing anything really definite in that direction till the family come. I thought I would just look around, meantime, in a quiet way, and make up my mind. Besides, I know a good many dead people, and I was calculating to hunt them up and swap a little gossip with them about friends, and old times, and one thing or another, and ask them how they like it here, as far as they have got. I reckon my wife will want to camp in the California range, though, because most all her departed will be there, and she likes to be with folks she knows."

"Don't you let her. You see what the Jersey district of heaven is, for whites; well, the Californian district is a thousand times worse. It swarms with a mean kind of leather-headed mud-colored angels—and your nearest white neighbor is likely to be a million miles away. *What a man mostly misses, in heaven, is company*—company of his own sort and color and language. I have come near settling in the European part of heaven once or twice on that account."

"Well, why didn't you, Sandy?"

"Oh, various reasons. For one thing, although you *see* plenty of whites there, you can't understand any of them, hardly, and so you go about as hungry for talk as you do here. I like to look at a Russian or a German or an Italian— I even like to look at a Frenchman if I ever have the luck to catch him engaged in anything that ain't indelicate—but *looking* don't cure the hunger—what you want is talk."

"Well, there's England, Sandy—the English district of heaven."

"Yes, but it is not so very much better than this end of the heavenly domain. As long as you run across Englishmen born this side of three hundred years ago, you are all right; but the minute you get back of Elizabeth's time the language begins to fog up, and the further back you go the foggier it gets. I had some talk with one Langland and a man by the name of Chaucer—old-time poets—but it was no use, I couldn't quite understand them, and they couldn't quite understand me. I have had letters from them since, but it is such broken English I can't make it out. Back of those men's time the English are just simply foreigners, nothing more, nothing less; they talk Danish, German, Norman French, and sometimes a mixture of all three; back of *them,* they talk Latin, and ancient British, Irish, and Gaelic; and then back of these come billions and billions of pure savages that talk a gibberish that Satan himself couldn't understand. The fact is, where you strike one man in the English settlements that you can understand, you wade through awful swarms that talk something you can't make head nor tail of. You see, every country on earth has been overlaid so often, in the course of a billion years, with different kinds of people and different sorts of languages, that this sort of mongrel business was bound to be the result in heaven."

"Sandy," says I, "did you see a good many of the great people history tells about?"

"Yes—plenty. I saw kings and all sorts of distinguished people."

"Do the kings rank just as they did below?"

"No; a body can't bring his rank up here with him. Divine right is a good-enough earthly romance, but it don't go, here. Kings drop down to the general level as soon as they reach the realms of grace. I knew Charles the Second very well—one of the most popular comedians in the English section—draws first rate. There are better, of course—people that were never heard of on earth—but Charles is making a very good reputation indeed, and is considered a rising man. Richard the Lion-hearted is in the prize-ring, and coming into considerable favor. Henry the Eighth is a tragedian, and the scenes where he kills people are done to the very life. Henry the Sixth keeps a religious book stand."

"Did you ever see Napoleon, Sandy?"

"Often—sometimes in the Corsican range, sometimes in the French. He always hunts up a conspicuous place, and goes frowning around with his arms folded and his field-glass under his arm, looking as grand, gloomy and peculiar as his reputation calls for, and very much bothered because he don't stand as high, here, for a soldier, as he expected to."

"Why, who stands higher?"

"Oh, a *lot* of people *we* never heard of before—the shoemaker and horse-doctor and knife-grinder kind, you know —clodhoppers from goodness knows where, that never handled a sword or fired a shot in their lives—but the soldiership was in them, though they never had a chance to show it. But here they take their right place, and Caesar and Napoleon and Alexander have to take a back seat. The greatest military genius our world ever produced was a bricklayer from somewhere back of Boston—died during the Revolution—by the name of Absalom Jones. Wherever he goes, crowds flock to see him. You see, everybody knows that if he had had a chance he would have shown the world some generalship that would have made all generalship before look like child's play and 'prentice work. But he never got a chance; he tried heaps of times to enlist as a private, but he had lost both thumbs and a couple of front teeth, and the recruiting sergeant wouldn't pass him. However, as I say, everybody knows, now, what he *would* have been, and so they flock by the million to get a glimpse of him whenever they hear he is going to be anywhere. Caesar, and Hannibal, and Alexander, and Napoleon are all on his staff, and ever so many more great generals; but the public hardly care to look at *them* when *he* is around. Boom! There goes another salute. The barkeeper's off quarantine now."[12]

Sandy and I put on our things. Then we made a wish, and in a second we were at the reception-place. We stood on the edge of the ocean of space, and looked out over the dimness, but couldn't make out anything. Close by us was the Grand Stand—tier on tier of dim thrones rising up toward the zenith. From each side of it spread away the tiers of seats for the general public. They spread away for leagues and leagues—you couldn't see the ends. They were empty and still, and hadn't a cheerful look, but looked dreary, like a theatre before anybody comes—gas turned down. Sandy says—

[12] ... Thousands of geniuses live and die undiscovered—either by themselves or others.... I have touched upon this matter in a small book which I wrote a generation ago and which I have not published as yet—*Captain Stormfield's Visit to Heaven.* When Stormfield arrived in heaven he was eager to get a sight of those unrivaled and incomparable military geniuses, Caesar, Alexander, and Napoleon, but was told by an old resident of heaven that they didn't amount to much there as military geniuses, that they ranked as obscure corporals only by comparison with a certain colossal military genius, a shoemaker by trade, who had lived and died unknown in a New England village and had never seen a battle in all his earthly life. He had not been discovered while he was in the earth, but heaven knew him as soon as he arrived there, and lavished upon him the honors which he would have received in the earth if the earth had known that he was the most prodigious military genius the planet had ever produced.

Bernard De Voto, *Mark Twain in Eruption*, p. 360.

"We'll sit down here and wait. We'll see the head of the procession come in sight away off yonder pretty soon, now."

Says I—

"It's pretty lonesome, Sandy; I reckon there's a hitch somewheres. Nobody but just you and me—it ain't much of a display for the barkeeper."

"Don't you fret, it's all right. There'll be one more gun-fire—then you'll see."

In a little while we noticed a sort of a lightish flush, away off on the horizon.

"Head of the torchlight procession," says Sandy.

It spread, and got lighter and brighter: soon it had a strong glare like a locomotive headlight; it kept on getting brighter and brighter till it was like the sun peeping above the horizon-line at sea—the big red rays shot high up into the sky.

"Keep your eyes on the Grand Stand and the miles of seats—sharp!" says Sandy, "and listen for the gunfire."

Just then it burst out, "Boom-boom-boom!" like a million thunderstorms in one, and made the whole heavens rock. Then there was a sudden and awful glare of light all about us, and in that very instant every one of the millions of seats was occupied, and as far as you could see, in both directions, was just a solid pack of people, and the place was all splendidly lit up! It was enough to take a body's breath away. Sandy says—

"That is the way we do it here. No time fooled away; nobody straggling in after the curtain's up. Wishing is quicker work than traveling. A quarter of a second ago these folks were millions of miles from here. When they heard the last signal, all they had to do was to wish, and here they are."

The prodigious choir struck up—

> We long to hear thy voice,
> To see thee face to face.

It was noble music, but the uneducated chipped in and spoilt it, just as the congregation used to do on earth.

The head of the procession began to pass, now, and it was a wonderful sight. It swept along, thick and solid, five hundred thousand angels abreast, and every angel carrying a torch and singing—the whirring thunder of the wings made a body's head ache. You could follow the line of the procession back, and slanting upward into the sky, far away in a glittering snaky rope, till it was only a faint streak in the distance. The rush went on and on, for a long time, and at last, sure enough, along comes the barkeeper, and then everybody rose, and a cheer went up that made the heavens shake, I tell you! He was all smiles, and had his halo tilted over one ear in a cocky way, and was the most satisfied-looking saint I ever saw.[13] While he marched up the steps of the Grand Stand, the choir struck up—

> The whole wide heaven groans,
> And waits to hear that voice

There were four gorgeous tents standing side by side in the place of honor, on a broad railed platform in the centre of the Grand Stand, with a shining guard of honor round about them. The tents had been shut up all this time. As the barkeeper climbed along up, bowing and smiling to everybody, and at last got to the platform, these tents were jerked up aloft all of a sudden, and we saw four noble thrones of gold, all caked with jewels, and in the two middle ones sat old white-whiskered men, and in the two others a couple of the most glorious and gaudy giants, with platter halos and beautiful armor. All the millions went down on their knees, and stared, and looked glad, and burst out into a joyful kind of murmurs. They said—

[13]MTP NB p. 51. Copyright The Mark Twain Company 1970. Wakeman—You talk about happy creatures—did you ever notice a porpoise?—Well there ain't anything in heaven here superior to that happiness. Put the Early Christian into the mouth of a poor fellow who is pathetic over his loss of it.

CAPTAIN STORMFIELD'S VISIT TO HEAVEN

"Two archangels!—that is splendid. Who can the others be?"

The archangels gave the barkeeper a stiff little military bow; the two old men rose; one of them said, "Moses and Esau welcome thee!" and then all the four vanished, and the thrones were empty.

The barkeeper looked a little disappointed, for he was calculating to hug those old people, I judge; but it was the gladdest and proudest multitude you ever saw—because they had seen Moses and Esau. Everybody was saying, "Did you see them?—I did—Esau's side face was to me, but I saw Moses full in the face, just as plain as I see you this minute."

The procession took up the barkeeper and moved on with him again, and the crowd broke up and scattered. As we went along home, Sandy said it was a great success, and the barkeeper would have a right to be proud of it forever.[14] And he said *we* were in luck, too; said we might attend receptions for forty thousand years to come, and not have a chance to see a brace of such grand moguls as Moses and Esau. We found afterwards that we had come near seeing another patriarch, and likewise a genuine prophet besides, but at the last moment they sent regrets. Sandy said there would be a monument put up there, where Moses and Esau had stood, with the date and circumstances, and all about the whole business, and travelers would come for thousands of years and gawk at it, and climb over it, and scribble their names on it.

---

[14]MTP NB #12. Nov. 23. 1877-78. Copyright The Mark Twain Company 1970. p. 4. March 20. Have all sorts of heavens—have a gate for each sort. One gate where they receive a barkeeper with artillery salutes, swarms of angels in the sky & a noble torch-light procession. *He* thinks he is *the* lion of Heaven. Procession over, he drops at once into awful obscurity, (& thinks this) But the roughest part of it is, that he has to do 30 weeks penance—one day and night he must carry a torch, & shout himself hoarse, to do honor to some poor scrub whom he wishes had gone to hell.

CHAPTER V

Captain Stormfield Resumes

I

WHEN I HAD BEEN in heaven some time I begun to feel restless, the same as I used to on earth when I had been ashore a month, so I sejested to Sandy that we do some excursions. He said all right, and with that we started with a whiz—not that you could *hear* us go, but it was as if you ought to.—On account of our going so fast, for you go by *thought*. If you went only as fast as light or electricity you would be forever getting to any place, heaven is so big. Even when you are traveling by thought it takes you days and days and days to cover the territory of any Christian State, and days and days and days to cover the uninhabited stretch between that State and the next one.

"You can't put it into miles," Sandy says.

"Becuz there ain't enough of them. If you had all the miles God ever made they wouldn't reach from the Catholic camp to the High Church Piscopalian—nor half way, for that matter; and yet they are the nearest together of any. Professor Higgins tries to work the miles on the measurements, on account of old earthly habit, and p'raps he gets a sort of grip on the distances out of the result, but you couldn't, and I can't."

"How do *you* know I couldn't, Sandy? Speak for yourself, hadn't you better? You just tell me his game, and wait till I look at my hand."

"Well, it's this. He used to be astronomical professor of astronomy at Harvard—"

"This was before he was dead?"

"Certainly. How could he be *after* he was dead?"

"Oh, well, it ain't important. But a *soldier* can be a soldier after he's dead. And he can breed, too. There's eleven million dead soldiers drawing pension at home, now—some that's been dead 125 years—and we've never had three millions on the pay-roll since the first Fourth of July. Go on, Sandy. Maybe it was before he was dead, maybe it wasn't; but it ain't important."

"Well, he was astronomical professor, and can't get rid of his habits. So he tries to figure out these heavenly distances by astronomical measurements. That is to say, he computes them in light-years."

"What is a light-year, Sandy?"

"He says light travels 186,000 miles a second, and—"

"How many?"

"186,000."

"In a *second*, Sandy—not a week?"

"No, in a second. He says the sun is 93,000,000 miles from the earth, and it takes light 8 minutes to cover the distance. Then he ciphers out how far the light would travel in a year of 365 days at that gait, and he calls that distance a light-year."

"It's considerable, ain't it, Sandy?"

"Don't you doubt it!"

"How far is it, Sandy?"

"It's 63,280 times the distance from the earth to the sun."

"Land! Say it again, Sandy, and say it slow."

"63,280 times 93,000,000 miles."

"Sandy, it beats the band. Do you think there's room for a straight stretch like that? Don't you reckon it would come to the edge and stick out over? What does a light-year foot up, Sandy, in a lump?"

"Six thousand million miles."

"Sandy, it is certainly a corker! Is there any known place as far off as a light-year?"

"Shucks, Stormy, *one* light-year is nothing. He says it's *four* light-years from our earth to the nearest star—and nothing between."

"*Nothing* between? Nothing but just emptiness?"

"That's it; nothing but emptiness. But he says there's not a star in the Milky Way nor anywhere else in the sky that's not *further* away from its nearest neighbor than that."

"Why, Sandy, if that is true, the sky is emptier than heaven."

"Oh, indeed, no! Far from it. In the Milky Way, the professor says, no star is more than six or seven light-years distant from its nearest neighbor, but there ain't any Christian sect in heaven that is nearer than 5,000 light-years from the camp of the next sect. Oh, no, he says the sky *is* a howling wilderness, but it can't show with heaven. No, sir, he says of all the lonesome places that ever was, give him heaven. Every now and then he gets so lonesome here that he makes an excursion amongst the stars, so's to have a sense of company."

"Why, Sandy, what have they made heaven so large for?"

"So's to have room in the future. The redeemed will still be coming for billions and billions and billions and billions of years, but there'll always be room, you see.[15] This heaven ain't built on any 'Gates Ajar' proportions."

... Time drifted along. We went on excursioning amongst the colonies and over the monstrous spaces between, till at last I was so weighed down by the awful bigness of heaven that I said I'd got to see something small to back my natural focus and lift off some of the load, I couldn't stand it any longer. Sandy says,

"Well, then, suppose we try an asterisk, or asteroid, or whatever the professor calls them. They're little enough to fit the case, I reckon."

[15][Scratched out]
"Yes, I hadn't thought of that. But there's no need of its being so lonesome, Sandy. Why don't they bunch the whole accumulation together?"
"How you talk, Stormfield! Do the denominations bunch together on earth? Catholics and heretics, for instance? Didn't they always burn each other when they could? Oh, heaven *would* be a Halifax of a place! If they bunched I wouldn't

II

Journey to the Asterisk

[Scratched out]

[(By and by it was getting dull again, and I said so, and Sandy says,

"We've excursioned to the other planets and looked them over—the big ones. Suppose we try an asterisk, or an asteroid,[16] or whatever the professor calls them.")][17]

[16]MTP NB   MTP NB (p. 26). p. 40. Nobody would go to Bunyan's heaven now, since our improvements have made this life attractive, but it was a superior place in his day. . . . Pay a visit to several old abandoned heavens—Bunyan's visited as a historical-theological Tower of London, but nobody willing to live in it.
MTP NB #14. Feb. 26, 1879-Sept. 8, 1879. p. 17. Wakeman says—it seemed an odd thing to me that we never received spirit communications from spirits born in the other stars.
MTP NB #12, Nov. 23, 1878-78. p. 4. March 20 Wakeman visits these various heavens. W. is years & years in darkness *between* solar systems.
MTP NB #12. Nov. 23, 1877-78. p. 15. Wakeman comes across Ollendorff & proceeds to learn the language of a near-lying district of Heaven—people of Jupiter? [(Cf SLC to WDH 6/27/78)]
[17]MTP NB #23 (II). p. 58. I found the astronomer of the University gadding around after çomets (& things) instead of attending to business. I told him pretty plainly that we couldn't have that. I told him (that) it was no economy to go on piling up raw material in the way of new stars & comets & trash that we couldn't ever have any use for till we had worked up the old stock. I said if I caught him scouring around after any more (of) asteroids, especially, I should have to scour him out of the place. Privately, prejudice got the best of me there, I ought to confess it. I don't mind comets, so much, but (from my earliest) somehow I never could stand
have always been down on asteroids. To my mind (they're only just)
                                                                whelps
there's nothing mature about them—only just pups out of some planet. Well,
                                                  they were just pie to him
then, of course it annoyed me to hear him say he preferred asteroids to anything else, & I said it was pretty degraded taste. (He said there was more money in it than in any other (line) of the business, because, he said astronomical real estate has its fluctu.) And I requested him to not talk back. I said it was pretty low-down business for great universities to be in—Rochester always raking the deeps of space for comet-spawn & trading it to Yale for (asteroids) planet-pups. Copyright The Mark Twain Company 1970.

[*101*]

So we went, and it was quite interesting. It was a very nice little world, twenty-five or thirty miles in circumference; almost exactly a thousand times smaller than the earth, and just a miniature of it, in every way: little wee Atlantic oceans and Pacific oceans and Indian oceans, all in the right places; the same with the rivers, the same with the lakes; the same old familiar mountain ranges, the same continents and islands, the same Sahara—all in the right proportions and as exact as a photograph. We walked around it one afternoon, and waded the oceans, and had a most uncommon good time. We spent weeks and weeks walking around over it and getting acquainted with the nations and their ways.

Nice little dollies, they were, and not bigger than Gulliver's Lilliput people. Their ways were like ours. In their America they had a republic on our own plan, and in their Europe, their Asia and their Africa they had monarchies and established churches, and a pope and a Czar, and all the rest of it. They were not afraid of us; in fact they held us in rather frank contempt, because we were giants. Giants have never been respected, in any world. These people had a quite good opinion of themselves, and many of them no bigger than a clothes pin. In church it was a common thing for the preacher to look out over his congregation and speak of them as the noblest work of God—and never a clothes pin smirked! These little animals were having wars all the time, and raising armies and building navies, and striving after the approval of God every way they could. And whenever there was a savage country that needed civilizing, they went there and took it, and divided it up among the several enlightened monarchs, and civilized it— each monarch in his own way, but generally with Bibles and bullets and taxes. And the way they did whoop-up Morals, and Patriotism, and Religion, and the Brotherhood of Man was noble to see.

I couldn't see that they differed from us, except in size.[18] It was like looking at ourselves through the wrong end of the spyglass. But Sandy said there was one difference, and a big one. It was this: each person could look right into every other person's mind and read what was in it, but he thought his own mind was concealed from everybody but himself![19]

---

[18]MTP NB #32b (II) Sept. 24, 1897-Aug. 1899 (p. 28). pp. 54-55. Missionary visit to Sirius. Write it over again. The stature is 9 to 10,000 feet high. When the missionary crawls across a page & passes the base of an h, the upper half towers above him like a factory chimney.
The air there holds him up—he falls like thistle-down & is not hurt. The glue of the spider web is not moist enough to stick to him—too coarse.
He is naked, of course—can't get clothes there.
Stormfield in Heaven—must write it over.
[19]MTP NB #17. p. 41. A friend of Wakeman in heaven gave his note for a thousand years & kept it up till he became embarrassed & his business went into the hands of a receiver. Copyright The Mark Twain Company 1970.

CHAPTER VI

From Captain Stormfield's Reminiscences

ONE DAY, whilst I was there in Heaven, I says to Sandy—"Sandy," I says, "you was telling me, a while back, that you knowed how the human race came to be created; and now, if you don't mind," I says, "I'd like you to pull off the narrative, for I reckon it's interesting."

So he done it. This is it.

Sandy's Narrative

Well, it was like this. I got it from Slattery. Slattery was there at the time, being an eye-witness, you see; and so Slattery, he—

"Who's Slattery, Sandy?"

One of the originals.

"Original *which?*"

Original inventions. He used to be an angel, in the early times, two hunderd thousand years ago; and so, as it happened—

"Two hun—do you mean to say—"

Yes, I *do*. It was two hunderd thousand years ago. Slattery was born here in heaven, and so time don't count. As I was a-telling you, he was an angel, first-off, but when Satan fell, he fell, too, becuz he was a connexion of Satan's, by marriage or blood or somehow or other, and it put him under suspicion, though they warn't able to prove anything on him. Still, they judged a little term down below in the fires would be a lesson to him and do him good, so they give him a thousand years down in them tropics, and—

"A *thousand,* Sandy?"

Certainly. It ain't anything to these people, Cap'n Stormfield. When you've been here as long as I have—but never mind about that. When he got back, he was different. The vacation done him good. You see, he had had experience, and it sharpened him up. And besides, he had traveled, and it made him important, which he warn't, before. Satan came near getting a thousand years himself, that time—

"But I thought he *did*, Sandy. I thought he went down for good and all."

No, sir, not that time.

"What saved him?"

Influence.

"M-m. So they have it here, too, do they?"

Oh, well, I sh'd *think!* Satan has fell a lot of times, but he hasn't ever been sent down permanent, yet—but only the small fry.

"Just the same it used to was, down on the earth, Sandy. Ain't it interesting? Go on. Slattery he got reinstated, as I understand it?"

Yes, so he did. And he was a considerable person by now, as I was a-saying, partly on accounts of his relative, and partly on accounts of him having been abroad, and all that, and affecting to talk with a foreign accent, which he picked up down below. So he was around when the first attempts was made. They had a mould for a man, and a mould for a woman, and they mixed up the materials and poured it in. They came out very handsome to look at, and everybody said it was a success. So they made some more, and kept on making them and setting them one side to dry, till they had about ten thousand. Then they blew in the breath, and put the dispositions in, and turned them loose in a pleasant piece of territory, and told them to go it.

"Put in the dispositions?"

Yes, the *Moral Qualities*. That's what makes dispositions. They distributed 'em around perfectly fair and honorable. There was 28 of them, according to the plans and specifications, and the whole 28 went to each man and woman in equal measure, nobody getting more of a quality than anybody else, nor less. I'll give you the list, just as Slattery give it to me:

1. Magnanimity.
2. Meanness.
3. Moral courage
4. Moral cowardice.
5. Physical courage.
6. Physical cowardice.
7. Honesty.
8. Dishonesty.
9. Truthfulness
10. Untruthfulness.
11. Love
12. Hate.
13. Chastity
14. Unchastity.
15. Firmness
16. Unfirmness.
17. Diligence
18. Indolence.
19. Selfishness.
20. Unselfishness.
21. Prodigality
22. Stinginess.
23. Reverence
24. Irreverence.
25. Intellectuality
26. Unintellectuality.
27. Self-Conceit
28. Humility.

"And a mighty good layout, Sandy. And all fair and square, too, and no favors to anybody. I like it. Looks to me elegant, and the way it had ought to be. Blamed if it ain't interesting. Go on."

Well, the new creatures settled in the territory that was app'inted for them, and begun to hatch, and multiply and replenish, and all that, and everything went along to the queen's taste, as the saying is. But by and by Slattery noticed something, and got Satan to go out there and take a look, which he done, and says,

"Well, something the matter, you think? What is it?"

"I'll show you," Slattery says. "Warn't they to be something fresh, something new and surprising?"

"Cert'nly," Satan says. "Ain't they?"

"Oh, well," says Slattery, "if you come right down to the

fine shades, I ain't able to deny that they *are* new—but *how* new? What's the idea? Moreover, what I want to know is, is what's new an *improvement?*"

"Go on," says Satan, a little impatient, "what's your point? Get at it!"

"Well, it's this. These new people don't differ from the angels. Except that they hain't got wings, and they don't get sick, and they don't die. Otherwise they're just angels—just the old usual thing. They're all the same size, they're all exactly alike—hair, eyes, noses, gait, everything—just the same as angels. Now, then, here's the point: the only solitary new thing about 'em is a new arrangement of their morals. It's the only fresh thing."

"Very well," says Satan, "ain't that enough? What are you complaining about?"

"No, it *ain't* enough, unless it's an improvement over the old regular arrangement."

"Come, get down to particulars!" says Satan, in that snappish way some people has.

"All right. Look at the old arrangement, and what do you find? Just this: the entire and complete and rounded-out sum of an angel's morals is *goodness*—plain, simple *goodness*. What's his equipment—a great long string of Moral Qualities with 28 specifications in it? No, there's only one—*love*. It's the whole outfit. They can't hate, they don't know how, becuz they can't help loving everything and everybody. Just the same, they don't know anything about envy, or jealousy, or avarice, or meanness, or lying, or selfishness, or *any* of those things. And so they're never unhappy, there not being any way for them to *get* unhappy. It makes *character*, don't it? And A1."

"Correct. Go on."

"Now then, look at these new creatures. They've got an immense layout in the way of Moral Qualities, and you'd think they'd have a stunning future in front of them—but it ain't so. For why? Because they've got Love *and* Hate, in the same proportions. The one neutralizes the other. They don't really love, and they don't really hate. They *can't,* you see. It's the same with the whole invoice: Honesty and Dishonesty, exactly the same quantity of each; selfishness and unselfishness; reverence and irreverence; courage and cowardice—and so on and so on. They are all exactly alike, inside and out, these new people—and *characterless.* They're ciphers, nothings, just waxworks. What do you say?"

"I see the point," says Satan. "The old arrangement was better."

Well, they got to talking around, and by and by others begun to see the point—and criticize. But not loud—only continuous. In about two hundred thousand years it got all around and come to be common talk everywheres. So at last it got to the Authorities.

"Would it take all that time, Sandy?"

"Here? Yes. It ain't long here, where a thousand years is as a day. It ain't six months, heavenly time. You've often noticed, in history, where the awful oppression of a nation has been going on eight or nine hundred years before Providence interferes, and everybody surprised at the delay. Providence *does* interfere, and mighty prompt, too, as you reconnize when you come to allow for the difference betwixt heavenly time and real time."

"By gracious I never thought of that before! I've been unfair to Providence a many and a many a time, but it was becuz I didn't think. Russia's a case in point; it looks like procrasination, but I see now, it ain't."

"Yes, you see, a thousand years earthly time being exactly a day of heavenly time, then of course a year of earthly time is only just a shade over a minute of heavenly time; and if you don't keep these facts in mind you are naturally bound to think Providence is procrasturing when it's just the other way. It's on accounts of this ignorance that many and many a person has got the idea that prayer ain't ever answered, and stuck to it to his dying day; whereas, prayer is *always* answered. Take praying for rain, f'instance. The prayer comes up; Providence reflects a minute, judges it's all right, and says to the Secretary of State, "turn it on." Down she comes, in a flood. But don't do any good of course, becuz it's a year late. Providence reflecting a minute has made all the trouble, you see. If people would only take the Bible at its word, and reconnize the difference betwixt heavenly time and earthly time, they'd pray for rain a year before they want it, and then they'd be all right. Prayer is always answered, but not inside of a year, becuz Providence has *got* to have a minute to reflect. Otherwise there'd be mistakes, on accounts of too much hurry."

"Why, Sandy, blamed if it don't make everything perfectly plain and understandable, which it never was before. Well, go on about what we was talking about."

"All right. The Authorities got wind of the talk, so they reckoned they would take a private view of them wax figures and see what was to be done. The end was, They concluded to start another Race, and do it better this time. Well, this was the Human Race."

"Wasn't the other the human race too, Sandy?"

"No. That one is neither one thing nor t'other. It ain't human, becuz it's immortal; and it ain't any account, becuz everybody is just alike and hasn't any character. The Holy Doughnuts—that is what they're called, in private."

"Can we go and see them some time, Sandy?" I says.

"Cert'nly. There's excursions every week-day. Well, the Authorities started out on the hypoetheneuse that the thing to go for in the new race was *variety*. You see, that's where the Doughnuts failed. Now then, was the Human Race an easy job? Yes, sir, it was. They made rafts of moulds, this time, no two of them alike—so there's your physical differentiations, till you can't rest! Then all They had to do was to take the same old 28 Moral Qualities, and mix them up, helter-skelter, in all sorts of different proportions and ladle them into the moulds—and there's your *dispositional* differentiations, b'George! Variety? Oh, don't mention it! Slattery says to me, 'Sandy,' he says, 'this dreamy old quiet heaven of ourn had been asleep for ages, but if that Human Race didn't wake it up don't you believe *me* no more!'

"Wake it up? Oh, yes, that's what it done. Slattery says the Authorities was awful suprised when they come to examine that Human Race and see how careless They'd been in the distribution of them Qualities, and the results that was a flowing from it.

" 'Sandy,' he says, 'there wasn't any foreman to the job, nor any plan about the distributing. Anybody could help that wanted to; no instructions, only look out and provide *variety*. So these 'commodating volunteers would heave a dipperful of Hate into a mould and season it with a teaspoonful of Love, and there's your *Murderer*, all ready for business. And into another mould they'd heave a teaspoonful of Chastity, and flavor it up with a dipperful of Unchastity—and so on and so on. A dipperful of Honesty and a spoonful of Dishonesty; a dipperful of Moral Courage and a spoonful of Moral Cowardice—and there's your splendid man, ready to stand up for an unpopular cause and stake his life on it; in another mould they'd dump considerable Magnanimity, and then dilute it down with Meanness till there wasn't any strength left in it—and so on and so on—the worst mixed-up mess of good and bad dispositions and half-good and half-bad ones a body could imagine— just a tagrag and bobtail Mob of nondescripts, and not worth propagating, of course; but what could the Authorities *do?* Not a thing. It was too late."

PART TWO

"The Late Reverend Sam Jones's Reception in Heaven"*

IT WAS the year 1897.

It had been a long, weary journey, and even in my sleep I was conscious of being almost willing to have it come to an end. Of course not quite willing,—considering the fate that was before me; that could not be expected. The long howl of the whistle bored its way into my drowsing ear, now, and as I came to myself the brakeman put his head in at the door and shouted the fatal words which so many of us had been daily expecting and dreading for many sad months:

"Noo-o-o Jer-roo-sa*lem!* Parties going through to Sheol please keep your seats, the rest step forward into the next car."

The misery in my heart was so heavy, so dull, so rayless, that the possibility of escape was an idea which could not have occurred to me. Yet escape was actually within my reach, as I perceived in the next moment! My former seat-mate was gone, and in his place sat a stranger of a most noble and benignant mien, tranquilly sleeping—a stranger whom I recognized without difficulty, from his published portraits: it was the Archbishop of Canterbury. He was traveling on a pass—a special, illuminated, gilt-edged personal pass—and had it in his hatband; for people with that kind of passes are easily tempted by the human nature in them to expose their high fortune to the view of the less for-

---

* Not published—forbidden by Mrs. Clemens.—S.L.C.

tunate. I had a pass too—also of a special and personal sort, but it was not the kind that one exhibits wantonly. With a feeling of humble and sincere gratitude I traded passes with the sleeper and moved into the forward car.

The train stopped, presently, and I stepped out onto the platform with the rest, but failed to get away in my turn, for a small person, clothed in a loud South-western costume, with a quid in his cheek and his wide-brimmed slouch hat tilted over his ear, elbowed me aside brusquely and went swaggering ashore whooping and screeching hosannahs like a demon.

But I was next, and glad I was to stand in the opaline glow of the pearly gates and realize that I was really there, though not expected. Only one person came from that other car. It was my substitute. I could not look him in the face, for at bottom I felt that my conduct had been doubtful. He stepped forward with a confidence which was pathetic to see, and turned his head about, this way and that, to let his pass be remarked—which it was, but the result was not reverence, but levity. That is, among the angels and other bystanders; St. Peter was not amused. To his mind this intrusion was a jest of poor quality and out of place. His manner was very cold. He said sternly to the Archbishop—

"Return to the train, sir. Professional humorists are not allowed here."

The unfortunate prelate was surprised and hurt. He drew himself up and said with some stiffness—

"It is evident that your Excellency does not recognize me. Permit me"—and he reached up for his pass and handed it to the offended saint with a barely perceptible bow. St. Peter made no motion to take it, but said with severity—

"Excuse me; although I do not recognize you, sir, I recognize your *nom de plume* with quite sufficient certainty, and must require you to make an end of this extraordinary impertinence and return at once to your train."

THE LATE REVEREND SAM JONES'S RECEPTION IN HEAVEN

"My *nom de plume!* Pardon me; Archbishop of Canterbury is a title, not a *nom de plume.*" This with a frozen bow.

It was all that St. Peter could do to keep his hands off of him.

"This is *too* much! That a person of your frivolous nature and profane instincts should conceive and carry out the daring jest of venturing across these sacred bounds was enough—quite enough; that you should add the affront of masquerading as an illustrious prelate whom all heaven is patiently waiting for and expecting to arrive today is—is—water!—give me water, before I choke!"

These words did not merely astonish the Archbishop, they stupefied him. He stood a moment or two like one in a dream, his eyes wandering vacantly about and resting nowhere; until at last they fell by chance upon the brimstone-tinted pass in his hand; then he murmured in a piteous voice, and as one distraught—

"Mark Twain?—Mark Twain? Alas, there has been some mistake."

Ah, he was humble, now, very humble, poor soul, and was about to plead with St. Peter to have pity on him and hear him try to account for the questionable situation he was in, but just at this point the riotous blather skite from the South-west came hosannahing up and shouldered him out of the way, shrieking exultantly—

"Glory and amen, Old Sam's *got* there!—hey, boys?" and he swept the circle of angels and elect with a joyous eye. To the Chief of the Apostles he exclaimed in his great voice, "*Know* me, hey?—I *bet* you do! Old Sam Jones—*Reverend* Sam Jones—old iron-bound brass-mouthed copper-bellied hell-smiter and Satan's-terror from the wilds of Texas! Shake!"

St. Peter shuddered, and kept his hand to himself. He said in his chill official voice—

"Exhibit your credentials, sir."

The man got his railroad ticket out of his wallet, and

the Apostle slowly and pains-takingly read the details on its back, reflected a good while, then read them again. He called an expert. The expert made a patient and particular examination and ended by pronouncing the ticket regular, also genuine. It was easy to see that St. Peter was disappointed and annoyed. He said to the expert—

"Can't you find *any* defect?"

"No, your Excellency; as far as the bald and sterile letter goes, it meets the requirements. There are several precedents; he will have to be accepted."

"Very well, then"—to the applicant—"you can enter. Wait —not here; go around the back way. And take off your arctics. Another thing: gag yourself until you are out of my hearing—This is not Texas. One of you go and show him where he can wash. Next!" He turned and saw the Archbishop of Canterbury starting for the train; he was touched, and said, gently: "Wait, poor clown; come back and sit down. I will look into your case presently, and give you every chance; and if you can prove that a mistake has been made I will let you in."

The Archbishop turned about eagerly—then stopped, hesitated a moment and said, with some little embarrassment in his manner—

"You are very kind—and indeed I thank your Excellency; but is—is he—going to remain?"

"Who?"

"He. The—the person from Texas."

"Why—well—he—well, the fact is—but *you* see how we are situated."

"Yes, I am afraid I do, your Excellency. I believe I will not tarry. Adieu!"

The conductor shouted—

"All aboard for Sheol!" and the train went spinning away. All its other passengers were crying, but the Archbishop was calm. I heard St. Peter mutter, absently—

"That is no humorist, that is a man of a sound cold judgment. In my opinion there has been a mistake here somewhere. Come,—just wait a moment, please. Who are *you*?" This to me, impatiently. It was a little sudden, and not altogether pleasant for me, for I was trying to glide in without verifying. I answered, with dignity, that I was the late Archbishop of Canterbury. That caught *him* a little sudden, but he used his miraculous powers and so nothing happened. *Others* laughed, though; that is, I suspected it was that at bottom, although to all outward appearances it was only a general outbreak of coughing. I have seen that kind of coughing before, and do not consider that there is anything either generous or polite about it. I was required to exhibit my credentials—my pass—and did it. There was a tedious long examination of it, and every effort made, as it seemed to me, to find something crooked about it. Meantime several angels talked me over in a quite free way, using the Chinese language, under the impression that I could not understand them. They spoke it very well, though with a slight foreign accent—a heavenly accent, and quite pretty.[1] One said he would not have taken me for an Archbishop. Another said no, he wouldn't either— thought I looked pretty rocky. A third said it was a pity— such unusual preparations had been made—they seemed hardly worth the candle. No. 1 said yes, the public were going to be disappointed in me, if he knew the tastes of the heavenly hosts, and he thought he did. No. 2 made a disparaging remark about the Texas rioter, coupling it with a like remark about me, and said it appeared to be a cold day for recruits. No. 3 said it was a grave mistake to let such characters in, it lowered the tone of the place *another* thirty or forty degrees. No. 2 thought the same; there had been a growing complaint and dissatisfaction about this sort of thing; in the opinion

[1] MTP NB #32a (I), Jan. 7, 1897-June 15, 1897, p. 23. "I have traveled more than any one else, and I have noticed that even the angels speak English with an accent." Copyright The Mark Twain Company 1970.

of some, the society of the other place was already preferable in some respects to the society here, on account of the presence among us of Pope Alexander VI, and Torquemade, and Catherine de' Medici and a too liberal number of others like them—and *now!* why these two break the record! Yes, No. 1 said, there had been ominous mutterings this long time; in his opinion there would be open revolt now; indeed he should not be surprised to see the better classes emigrate. This embarrassing and ill-bred talk was still going on when the expert announced that my ticket was undeniably straight; whereupon St. Peter said to me with much unfriendliness in his tone—

"You can enter in, sir, I am not able to help it; but if I could have had my way I would have made short work of you and that Texan bandit."

I was there a week, and I pledge my word that I led a modest and inoffensive life and did the best I could to please the people; but they were prejudiced and said I had always been a light speaker and they could not abide such things. Now in sober truth I never had said anything half as bad as some ministers had been allowed to say and no fault found. But there was just the difference— I was a layman, you see, and not privileged to blaspheme; coarse speeches were permissible in some mouths, but not in all.

Sam Jones was preaching and exhorting and carrying on all the time, and in the sincerest and most heartfelt way, too, but it was in language that made the place fairly shudder; so the dissatisfaction was immediate and pronounced. Even the papal Borgias were revolted. The exodus began on the Monday morning early: there was a panic, and a universal break for the under-world. When the gates closed, Saturday night, the Texan had the place all to himself.

Mark Twain

PART THREE

"Mental Telegraphy?"*

IT REALLY LOOKS LIKE IT. Last night I listened with great and peculiar interest to the reading of a sketch by Bernard Shaw which is about to appear in Collier's Weekly. It was an account of the translation to heaven of a dissipated old woman of the hard-working class, and some of her experiences there.[1]

Once I wrote an account of the translation to heaven of an uneducated and uncultivated old seaman, and certain of his experiences there. This was thirty or forty years ago. I began the article forty or forty-one years ago as a good-natured satire upon "The Gates Ajar," a book which everybody was reading in those days, but I did not finish it. Twelve or fifteen years later I finished it and read it to Mr. Howells, who wanted it published, and said he believed Dean Stanley would shore it up with an introduction.

---

* Written November 1907—DV #254.

[1] *Collier's, The National Weekly.* Saturday November 23, 1907, pp. 12-13. Meek Mrs. Hairns, a drunken charwoman arrives at the gate of heaven at same time as the Bishop of St. Pancras. She is cheerfully greeted by St. Peter and the other angels at the gate, who invite her in to heaven. She wonders if she is worthy to enter, but they assure her that all are welcome. She still is reluctant to enter. The Bishop blusters his way in, looking for God and His Throne. He lets it be known immediately that he finds it intolerable that all enter by the same gate, that heaven seems to be a democracy. St. Peter and others spoof him, have fun at his expense, generally humiliate him. He gets angry and blusters off, but soon returns thinking that perhaps it would be politic to be nice to God's angels. Finally he unbends and starts playing football with the angels. When all the angels are busy playing football, Mrs. Hairns slips into Heaven unnoticed. "As her foot approached the threshold the houses of the heavenly street shone friendly in the sunshine before her, and the mosaics in the pavement glowed like flower-beds of jewels."

But I pigeon-holed it. Now and then, as the years and decades drifted by, I took out the article and glanced through it with an eye to printing it, but always concluded to wait a while longer, and let it finish ripening.

Several months ago I examined it again. It seemed to be about ripe, so I sent it to Harper's Monthly, for the Christmas number, labeling it "Captain Stormfield's Visit to Heaven." Three weeks ago I read and revised the proofs, and struck out one or two of the Captain's adventures, and by to-day the magazine is printed and waiting for delivery-day. Last night Mr. Shaw's article reminded me, several times, of my own, particularly in treatment—a flowing, free-handed treatment, not much embarrassed by shopworn conventions. This resemblance, taken by itself, could not suggest mental-telegraphic origin, but there were several striking details that did strongly suggest it. So I said "Mr. Shaw must have gotten those incidents out of my head when I was in England last summer, by thought-transference, for there was no talk of my article, and neither it nor any detail of it was mentioned to him."

But suppose those incidents were *not* in my article—what then? Upon reflection I found that that was indeed the case —they were not there, and to my sorrow the pleasant mental-telegraphy theory began to crumble to ruin. I say to my regret, because ever since a certain remarkable episode of about 1875 (recounted in one of my books), I have been a confirmed and stubborn believer in mental telegraphy— the unconscious transference of inventions, ideas, phrases, paragraphs, chapters, and even entire books, from mind to mind—so strong a believer in it, indeed, that I am now not able to believe that I often originate ideas in my mind but get almost all of them out of somebody else's by unconscious and uninvited thought-transference.

As I have said, there were incidents in Mr. Shaw's article which I recognized as mine, yet they were not in "Captain Stormfield's Visit to Heaven:" where, then, were they? The answer presently dawned dimly above the horizon of my memory, then rose bright and clear: they were in a never-printed extravaganza which I wrote in Germany seventeen years ago, entitled "The Late Rev. Sam Jones's Reception In Heaven." And so my tottering mental-telegraphy edifice stiffened promptly up, from cellar to lightning rod.

I was ever so fond of that "Reception" article, and dearly wanted to print it, but it was hilarious and extravagant to the very verge of impropriety, and I could not beguile my wife into consenting to its publication. In that day Sam Jones was sweeping the South like a cyclone with his revival meetings, and converting the unconverted here and there and everywhere with his thundering torrents of piety and slang. I represented him as approaching the New Jerusalem in the through express, and in the same pullman in which he and his feet together were occupying two chairs, sat his grace the late Archbishop of Canterbury (Mr. Tait), and I.

APPENDIX A

Old Abe's "Slap" at Chicago*

"Old Abe's 'Slap' at Chicago" (pp.114-16)
Mr. Lincoln relates the following:

Some years ago, when Chicago was in its infancy, a stranger took up his quarters at the principal hotel, and inscribed his name on the register as Mr. J—————, of St. Louis. For several days he remained there, engaged in transacting the business which had brought him to the place, and from his exceedingly plain dress, manners and general appearance, attracted but little attention.

Soon Mr. J————— was suddenly seized with illness, during which he was sadly neglected by his host; and the servants taking their tone from the master of the house, left him to shift for himself as best he could. Then matters went on, till one morning he was past praying for; his papers were then examined, that the sad intelligence might be communicated to his friends; when to the surprise of all he was found to be one of the wealthiest men in the western country.

Arrangements were accordingly made for the funeral; but before the last rites were performed, the subject came to life again, having been the victim of catalepsy, instead of the grim 'King of Terror.' All were overjoyed at his fortunate excape from so dreadful a fate, and from that time were profuse in their expressions of solicitude, elicited, however, we judge, by 'documentary evidence', rather than by any personal regard.

* *Old Abe's Jokes: Fresh from Abraham's Bosom. Containing all his issues, Excepting the "greenbacks."* To call in some of which, this work is issued. New York. T. R. Dawley. Cop. 1864.

At length some one ventured to ask, how things appeared to him while in his trance, to whom he thus replied.

'I thought I had come to the river of death, where I met an angel who handed me a jewel to serve as a pass to the other side. On giving this to the ferryman, I received from him another which carried me further another stage in my journey. Going on thus for several stages, receiving at the termination of each, a ticket for the succeeding one, I at last reached the gate of the Heavenly City. There I found St. Peter, who opened the door at my summons, pipe in mouth, seated by a small table, on which stood a goodly mug of steaming whiskey toddy.

"Good morning, sir," said he very politely.

"Good morning, St. Peter," said I.

"Who are you, sir?" said he, turning over the leaves of a huge ledger.

"My name is J——."

"Very good, sir; where do you live down below?"

"I lived in St. Louis, in the state of Missouri."

"Very well, sir: and where did you die?"

"I died in Chicago, in Illinois."

"Chicago?" said he, shaking his head, "there's no such place, sir."

"I beg your pardon, St. Peter, but have you a map of the United States here?"

"Yes, sir."

"Allow me to look at it."

"Certainly, sir."

With that he handed down a splendid atlas, and I pointed out Chicago on the map.

"All right, sir;" said he after a moment's pause; "it's there, sure enough, so walk in, sir; but I'll be blest if you ain't the first man who ever came here from that place!"

Thus ended Mr. J——'s account of his transition state; and no more questions were asked.

APPENDIX B

Alternate Passage

... you are playing the mischief with it in another."

"As How?"

"Well, for instance. You make the baby *grow up*—you make the young girl and the young man progress along into age, and *take on the look of it and the signs of it!* My land, it chilled me all through to think of it! Imagine a sweet young mother seeing her little baby die, twenty years ago, and keeping her heart from breaking by saying a million times, through her tears, 'I shall see my darling again in heaven'—and imagine that mother soaring into this place now, crazy to get that child in her arms again—and suppose—"

"Sh!—hold still," says Sandy, "I've seen it a hundred times. I had an instance last week. Mildred Rushmore—neighbor of ours, below—lost a baby sixteen months old, a couple of years before I died. It was her first—she was about twenty-five years old—& it seemed as if she would go stark mad with the grief of it. It would have broken anybody's heart to see the poor thing, & hear her wail & cry. All the comfort she could get was out of those very words, 'I shall see my child in heaven—I shall see her in heaven, & there we'll meet to part no more forever'—& then she would break down and cry again.

"Well, Mildred died in her own good time, and last week she arrived here. I was passing by that house yonder when I heard the whir of wings, and down she lit by me & fell flat. I lifted her up, brushed her off. She had recognized me, but I couldn't make her out till she told me who she was, for she is over fifty now, & pretty gray, whereas she was plump & young when I died.

"She was all aglow, her eyes were dancing. 'My child!' she says, 'take me to my child! O, take me to my baby, take me to my darling!'

"Just at that minute, out of that house steps a woman of about thirty, with five children following behind her.

"'This is your baby,' says I—'Your daughter, I mean—She is Mrs. McLaughlin, now, & these are her children.'

"The poor old thing stopped stock still, her eyes stared as glassy as a corpse's, & her wings drooped till they trailed the ground; never did I see anybody so stricken. She moaned out—

"'*This* my sweet lost baby!—O, there is some dreadful mistake, some cruel mistake!—Take me back to the grave—O, please, I cannot bear to live.'

"The other lady looked wonderingly & pityingly at her, as one would look at a harmless strange madman, & was about to move on.

"'Wait a minute,' says I, 'wait a minute, Mrs. McLaughlin, let me introduce you; this is your mother—the late Mrs. Rushmore.'

"'*My* mother?' she said, opening her kind eyes wide, but sort of half shrinking back, as if she judged it was a mistake or a joke.

"Mrs. Rushmore burst out crying, & fell limp in my arms, saying over & over again,—

"'O, why did I die? I wish I had never died! Go away, woman, I cannot bear you! Give me my child, O, give me my child!'

"It was very embarrassing to us all. Mrs. McLaughlin said in a hurt voice,—

"'Do not speak so to me, madam, I have never done you any harm. I do not know you, I have not heard of you before. Trouble has disordered your mind; but if you will come in my house I will do all I can to comfort you. And do

APPENDIX

not grieve, nor be afraid, poor lady, for here in heaven you cannot be unhappy long.'

"But Mrs. Rushmore waved her away & would not look at her, but went on wailing & begging to be taken to her child. So presently Mrs. McLaughlin went away with her children, on some business, whatever it was, & I took Mrs. Rushmore to my house."

"Is that all? What happened afterwards?"

"O well, what always happens. The two women got acquainted, & visited a little, for a day or so & called each other mother & daughter, & all that, but nothing came of it. They were strangers, & hadn't anything in common. Mrs. McLaughlin had been head over heels in astronomy for years, & didn't care to talk about anything else, whereas her poor old mother didn't know one star from t'other, & didn't want to. So of course they drifted apart inside of four days. They haven't any sympathies that they can hitch to—inside of a month they'll stop this fol-de-rol & just be acquaintances, nothing more."

"Well, but goodness! what will this poor old woman do, all alone in heaven? She can't be happy here, of course, after such a disappointment?"

"O, but can't she, though? She is already happy. She has raked up twenty or thirty friends & relations who died within two or three years before she did & it would have done your heart good to see these old cronies meet again. She has raked up her husband, too—he died about five years ahead of her. Happy? there ain't anybody in these realms that is happier than Mrs. Rushmore. She has got acquainted with a lot of simple-minded, harmless, ignorant Jersey people,—regular gossips—& they get together every day & pull other people's reputations to pieces, & slander the elect in general, wholesale & retail, & have a noble good time. Much she will be bothering about her lost child a month from now!"

"No, but do they really deal in that kind of gossip in heaven?"

"How you talk! Would heaven be heaven if you couldn't slander folks?"

"Come to think, I don't believe it would—for some people—but I hadn't thought of it before."

"For 'some people.'—There you hit it. The trouble on earth is, that they leave out the *some-people* class—they try to fix up a heaven for only one kind of people. It won't work. There's all kinds here—& God cares for all kinds. He makes all happy; if he can't do it in one way, he does it in another. He doesn't leave anybody out in the cold."